WAP

in ea

MIKE MCGRATH

in easy steps is an imprint of Computer Step
Southfield Road . Southam . Warwickshire CV47 OFB . England
Tel: +44 (0)1926 817999   Fax: +44 (0)01926 817005

www.ineasysteps.com

Notice of Liability

Every effort has been made to ensure that this book contains accurate and current information. However, Computer Step and the author shall not be liable for any loss or damage suffered by readers as a result of any information contained herein.

Trademarks

All trademarks are acknowledged as belonging to their respective companies.

Printed and bound in the United Kingdom

ISBN 1-84078-112-2

Contents

Introducing WAP

Welcome to Wireless Application Protocol (WAP). This first chapter discusses why the WAP standard has been created and how the Wireless Markup Language (WML) and WMLScript operate in the WAP environment. You'll also discover how you can use freely available WAP emulators to create and test your own WAP applications.

Covers

Chapter One

Why WAP?

The popularity of digital wireless user-agents has seen staggering growth in recent years with a massive global increase in the use of mobile phones. The addition of further capabilities means that the mobile phone is no longer merely a telephone but a communication device capable of running applications and communicating with other devices and applications over a wireless network.

WAP is the development of established Internet protocols and concepts intended to standardize the way in which pagers, mobile phones, and personal digital assistants (PDAs) access information and services.

The WAP specification is being developed by a democratic consortium called the WAP Forum which is backed by around 90% of the mobile telephone industry. You can see the latest specification developments on the WAP Forum Website at http://www.wapforum.com.

This diagram illustrates how applications are converted to travel between the host and the client in the WAP environment. The WAP emulator simulates the actions of both the WAP gateway and the WAP-enabled phone.

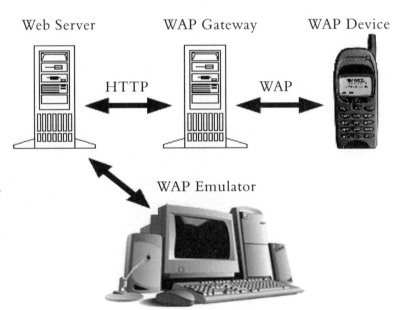

Web Server   WAP Gateway   WAP Device

HTTP   WAP

WAP Emulator

A Web server must have a WAP gateway to host WAP services.

A simple WAP application consists of files, located on a Web server, written in Wireless Markup Language (WML) and possibly script files written in WMLScript and graphic files in WMLBitmap format.

The WAP specifications for the client-side provide a layered communication protocol, which is embedded into each WAP-enabled phone, while the server-side uses a gateway through which the application server can communicate with the mobile phone. The gateway is an essential ingredient. It is used to binary encode the WAP content for optimum use of the networks.

How the Wireless Application Protocol works:

1 The user presses a phone key that has a URL assigned to it.

2 The phone sends a URL request to a WAP gateway using the WAP protocol.

3 The gateway creates a conventional HTTP request for the specified URL and sends it to the Web server.

4 The HTTP request is processed by the server. The URL may refer to a static WAP file or may use a CGI script to create the WAP content. The server will fetch the file and add a HTTP header to it, or if the URL specifies a script application, the server will run the script.

5 The Web server returns the WML content with the added HTTP header.

6 The WAP gateway verifies the HTTP header, and the WML content, then encodes them into binary form. The gateway then creates a WAP response containing WML and sends it to the phone.

7 The phone receives the WAP response and processes the WML to display the appropriate content.

Origins of WML

Wireless Markup Language (WML) is a markup language enabling the formatting of text in the WAP environment using a variety of markup tags to determine the display appearance of content. It is defined using the rules of eXtensible Markup Language (XML) and is therefore an XML application.

WML also provides a means of allowing the user to navigate around the WAP application and supports the use of anchored links as found commonly in Web pages.

Similar to the Hypertext Markup Language (HTML) used to format text in Web browsers, WML has been specially designed for use within the stricter confines of narrow-band mobile devices bearing these characteristics:

*   Small low-resolution display screens where typically each line can only contain 8-12 characters

*   Slower low-power CPUs and small memory capacity

*   Restrictions on power resources by not having mains supply

*   Limited input capabilities where a keyboard and mouse may not be present

*   A high round-trip latency (delay) where WAP requests may take 5-10 seconds

WML provides support for images and layout within the constraints of the device and permits the use of variables within strings to make the most efficient use of network resources.

The WML source files are located on the Web server and transported using Hypertext Transfer Protocol (HTTP) to the WAP gateway. Here the gateway compiles the WML into byte code and then transmits it using Wireless Application Protocol (WAP) to the device.

The WAP Forum is also responsible for the evolution of the WML specifications.

Adding WMLScript

The WMLScript language is based on ECMAScript and is similar to Javascript but designed specifically to add functionality to the static content of WML. For example, it allows validation of user input into a WAP application.

A smaller language is easier to learn than a big one.

WMLScript is optimised for efficiency in the WAP environment by omitting some of the more advanced features of ECMAScript in order to keep the language compact.

An important feature of WMLScript is the use of client-side libraries that are held resident in the phone in order to minimize the size of the WMLScript code that is needed.

A WMLScript unit may contain pragmas to specify information to the WMLScript compiler and any number of WMLScript functions as required by the WAP application.

In order to handle the WMLScript byte code the WAP-enabled device contains an interpreter to execute the WMLScript functions as they are called.

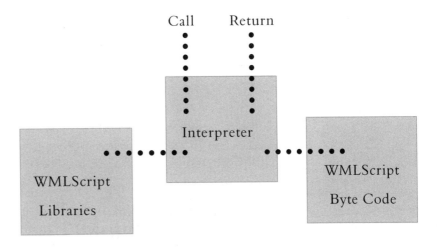

The operation works by running the downloaded WMLScript byte code and making reference to the intrinsic WMLScript libraries. The interpreter then returns the results of that function call for use in the application.

Nokia WAP Toolkit

The Nokia WAP emulator from Finland is available for free download after you register at the Nokia Forum Website at http://www.forum.nokia.com and consists of an executable file of 6.80 Mb. The Nokia WAP Toolkit is a Java-based application that needs you to have the Java Runtime Environment (JRE) installed of version 1.2.2 or later. This is available at http://www.javasoft.com and is a free download.

The Nokia documentation is in PDF format which requires Adobe Acrobat Reader which again is freely available from Adobe at http://www.adobe.com

When you start the Nokia WAP Toolkit you see that the user interface has a mobile phone simulator in the right-hand window. This is the WAP browser used to view WAP content as it would appear after transmission.

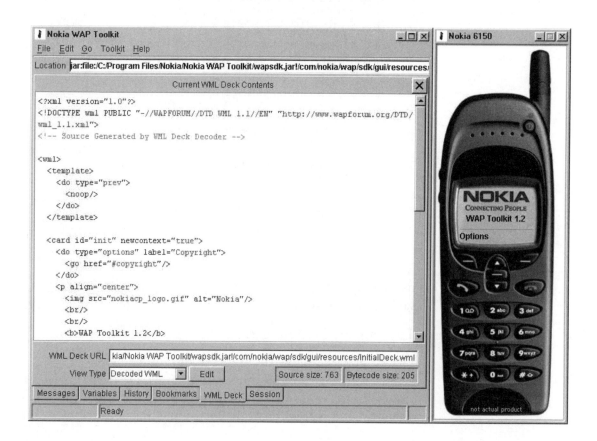

The other window contains a text editor to create and edit WML content. Clicking File|New on the toolbar reveals an option menu where you can opt to create a new WML file, or a new WMLScript file. The selected option opens a new tabbed editor window with some skeleton code included.

WAP has its own format for graphic image files which is the WML bitmap (.WBMP) and the Nokia Toolkit editor has an option to create these too in a new editor window containing drawing tools.

You can import GIF and JPG images, then convert them to WBMP files.

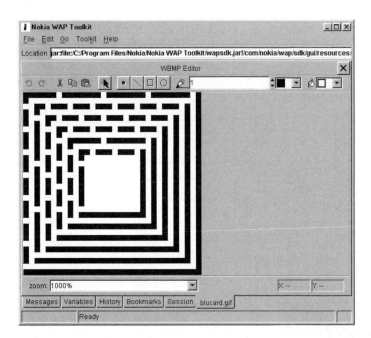

The Nokia WAP Toolkit is simple and straightforward to use saving new WML files with the file extension .WML, and saving new WMLScript files with the file extension .WMLS.

To simulate the WAP gateway both types of files are compiled into byte code by simply pressing the Compile button in the editor. The Nokia WAP Toolkit then creates new compiled files with the file extension .WMLC for WML files and .WMLSC for WMLScript files.

Ericsson WapIDE

The emulator from the Swedish manufacturer Ericsson is available for free download after registering on the Ericsson WAP Developers' Zone at http://www.ericsson.com/wap. The WapIDE is supplied in two-parts totalling 10.4 Mb and they must be installed in the correct order.

Selecting AppDesigner from the Launch menu opens the WapIDE user interface which consists of a Source editor for creating WML and WMLScript text files and a Device window for testing work in progress together with an Output window for application messages.

The Source editor has the option of inserting standard parts of WML code from Edit|Insert in the Source window toolbar. In practice it may be preferable to type code directly into the editor, although the Insert dialog boxes are useful when first starting with WML.

Code is easily compiled using the button on the Source window toolbar to create byte code files. You can quickly test your code using a button on the AppDesigner window toolbar to toggle between Edit mode and Test mode where your code automatically runs in the device window.

The Ericsson WapIDE saves your newly created files in a project. The project's main file has a .WAP extension and contains details of all other files within the project. A WML folder is automatically created within the project directory to hold WML (.WML) and WMLScript (.WMLS) files associated with the project in both text and compiled binary formats (.WMLC and .WMLSC).

There is also a device folder to house device-related files and a cgi-bin folder for server-side scripts.

A separate Browser is available from the Launch menu to view WAP content from a WAP internet site, your local system or through the freeware Xitami Web server included with the WapIDE.

The Server Toolset on the Launch menu includes a useful-sounding WML analyser tool, but this does not verify code.

No special attention is given to graphic files with the WapIDE and there is no WBMP editor in this package.

The Ericsson WapIDE may be rather more quirky to use than the Nokia WAP Toolkit and it is simpler to open the WML files directly instead of using those .WAP project files. It is still well thought-out and is a more complete package overall having the Web-server and libraries included.

Motorola ADK

The Motorola emulator from the United States of America is available for free download from the Motorola Website at http://mix.motorola.com.

The emulator is offered both with and without support for Microsoft Agent and the full version weighs in at 18.3Mb with supporting PDF documentation adding another 1.72Mb.

Before downloading this emulator please note the system requirements as the version that I tried will not install where the system has less than 64Mb of memory.

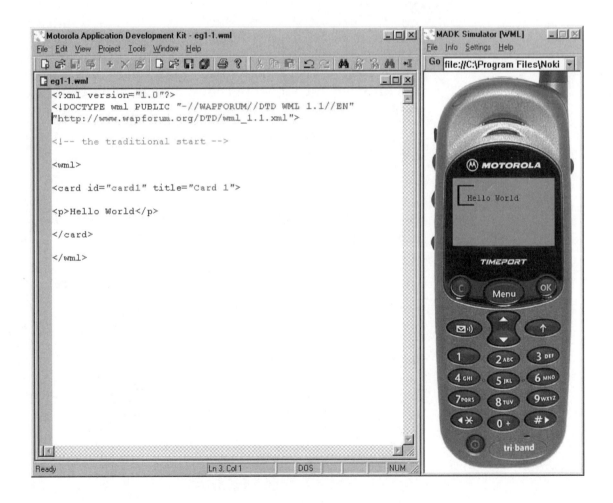

The Motorola ADK needs the support of the Microsoft Java Virtual Machine which is usually installed with recent versions of Microsoft Internet Explorer or can be downloaded from http://www.microsoft.com/java.

The Motorola emulator has added support for a voice markup language called 'voxml' which the Microsoft Agent support is intended to demonstrate.

There are a variety of imaginative configurations for the phone simulator but quite a few confusingly use the left and right arrow keys to scroll the display up or down.

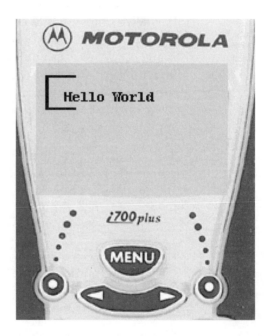

The version that I tried does not have the same level of compliance to the WML standard in many areas so is mentioned here only for completeness. The WAP content examples used throughout this book and illustrations all relate to the Nokia or Ericsson emulators.

Check the Motorola Website regularly for a new release with added support and news of recent developments.

Using WAP Emulators

Always accept the suggested locations when installing an emulator.

In order to develop WAP applications it is most convenient to use a WAP emulator. These are freely available from manufacturers of mobile phones and avoid the need to use an actual gateway to test the application you are developing.

The raw WML code is compiled into byte code by the built-in compiler so that the output can be viewed in a simulated phone and the application tested as it would appear in live use. All emulators stress that you should always run a final test in working conditions because there may be some deviations between the real environment and the simulated environment of the emulator.

The WML and WMLScript contained within this book have been run on both the Nokia Wap Toolkit and the Ericsson WapIDE. While both emulators are set to conform to the current WAP standard there are differing levels of implementation of the standard, so examples of output are given in this book to illustrate cases where the implementation of the WAP standard may vary.

Both emulators are built for the Windows operating system using either Windows 95 or later, and Windows NT4 with SP3 installed. They are designed for use at a resolution of 1024 x 768 and you will need around 20Mb of disk space. You should also have a Pentium-class processor of 266MHz or faster, and at least 64Mb of memory for best results.

Switch on the Ericsson phone when you start the Browser.

The mobile phone simulators are both very realistic and the Ericsson WapIDE Browser even requires you to switch the phone on each time you use it – this can be infuriating.

As the manufacturers add more compliance to meet the WAP standard further versions of their emulators will be released so you should frequently check their Websites to get the latest editions and find out the most recent developments.

- Nokia is at http://www.forum.nokia.com

- Ericsson is at http://www.ericsson.com/wap

- Motorola is at http://mix.motorola.com

Starting In WML

This chapter is an introduction to the basics of Wireless Markup Language (WML) and demonstrates the layout and requirements of WML documents. You will learn how to position text content on the display and how to change its appearance to suit your needs.

Covers

Chapter Two

Using the Browser

The browsers found in WAP emulators vary in design to reflect the way that actual phones have different interfaces.

The WML functionality is only loosely connected to the display leaving phone designers free to support the functions in different ways.

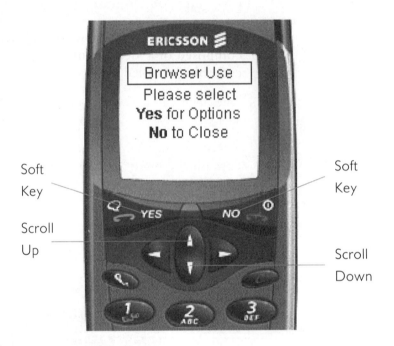

Soft keys are used to select from a menu of options.

Normally it is the left-hand soft key that is used to bring up the menu and select the options while the right-hand soft key returns you to the previous screen.

The arrow keys scroll the display in the direction of the arrow.

The user can enter input into the application using the alphanumeric keys. The application determines if letters or numbers are required. In the case of letter input, quickly pressing a key will scroll through the choice of letters available on that key.

Decks and Cards

Wireless Markup Language (WML) is a descriptive markup language used to determine the appearance of content by use of instructional tags similar to those found in HTML.

The tags can contain further attributes that may associate the marked-up content with particular tasks.

Let's start with a first look at WML in action.

Firstly, you need to know that a WML document is composed of a 'deck' containing data that is grouped into code blocks called "cards".

The deck can contain many cards and each card will display as a single page on the display screen.

The user can navigate through the cards by using the soft keys on the phone to follow links contained in each card. This is similar to following local document links in a Web page and the WML links even use the same familiar #label syntax to refer to a card.

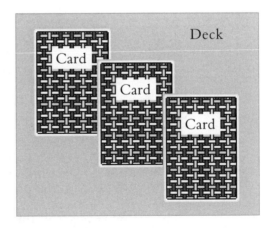

The deck is the WML file loaded into the phone when a URL is called and the contents of the first card within that deck will be displayed on the screen after the WML content has been validated.

Hello World

A single deck with a single card is the smallest unit of WML data which can be sent from a server to a user device, so we can start by looking at this simple deck:

The following WML code below is used to create the interface displays shown above:

```
<?xml version= "1.0"?>

<!DOCTYPE wml PUBLIC "-//WAPFORUM//DTD WML 1.1/
/EN" "http://www.wapforum.org/DTD/wml_1.1.xml">

<!— the traditional start —>

<wml>

<card id= "card1" title= "Card 1">

<p>Hello World</p>

</card>

</wml>
```

Let's run through this code to analyse it line by line.

The first line of code is required at the start of every WML file to declare the document to be a valid XML file. This is followed by the other declaration which you must have in every WML file to declare the document type.

Next is a comment line which is useful to add notes into the WML code for reference purposes.

All comments should begin with a <!— start tag and finish with a —> end tag and may cover multiple lines. Anything between the start and end tags will be ignored when the code is parsed for display.

The <wml> </wml> element tags surround the entire deck content and contain the various cards that may be used in the deck.

The <card> </card> element tags surround the card content and contain all the code used in that card. They include the 'id' attribute to give the card an identity for use by the code and a 'title' attribute to assign a name to be displayed on the screen.

Many tags have additional attributes with which you may specify values. You must always enclose the attribute values in double quotes ("...") in the code.

The actual text content for this card and deck is surrounded by the <p> </p> paragraph tags.

Paragraphs

The <p> element paragraph tags are required to enclose all text content and may include attributes to set the text alignment to left, right or center as in this example:

```
<wml>
<card id= "card1" title= "P Align">
<p align= "left">Left</p>
<p align= "center">Center</p>
<p align= "right">Right</p>
</card>
</wml>
```

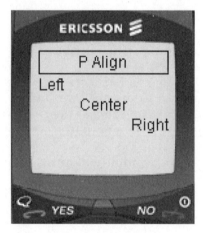
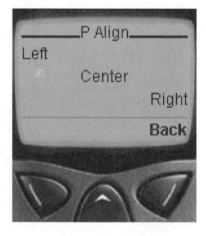

The paragraph tag may also include attributes to set the line-wrap mode to wrap or nowrap although the default mode (if not specified) is wrap. For example:

<p mode= "nowrap">This is text without line-wrap</p>

If nowrap is set then lines that exceed the visible display area may be truncated to display only a part of the text.

Formatting Text

There are a number of tag elements available in WML to format how text will be displayed on-screen.

The tags are used by placing a starting tag in front of the text to be formatted and a closing tag for that instruction at the end of the text:

- \
 is used to set a line break and is called an empty element because it will not contain any content. Empty element tags are single tags with a closing forward slash

- \<big> renders the text in a larger font

- \<small> reduces the text to a smaller font size

- \<em> displays the text with emphasis

- \<b> produces bold text

- \<i> renders the text in an italic font

- \<strong> creates text with strong emphasis

- \<u> underlines the text in the display – in a similar way to the way that hyperlinks are displayed on-screen

Avoid use of the underline tag to prevent confusion of underlined text with underlined hyperlinks.

Multiple formatting tags may be employed but care should be taken to nest the tags correctly. For example:

\<b>\<i>This is bold italic text wrongly nested\</b>\</i>

should be:

\<b>\<i>This is bold italic text correctly nested\</i>\</b>

Text Variance

There are unfortunate differences in the way that makers are implementing the WML standard with regard to text formatting tags.

The Nokia implementation seems to adhere most closely to the standard inasmuch as all the formatting tags do operate as they are supposed to.

Ericsson only support a single font so are unable to comply with the <big> <small> and <i> markup commands.

 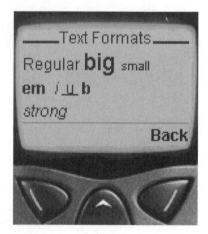

There is also a difference in the way that the <strong> markup command is treated.

The Nokia example on the right interprets <strong> to be italic whereas Ericsson make <strong> markup text both bold and underlined. In this case the underline with the <strong> tag has the same potential to confuse with displayed links so is best avoided.

So with the Ericsson implementation you really only usefully have the choice between bold or plain text, but this lack of options does help to reduce the WML byte code.

Using the Card Title

It is important when writing code for narrowband devices to remember the limitations of capacity and display size. The aim should be to utilise every pixel to best advantage with the minimum of code for fastest execution. Our simplest deck example wastes the space afforded by the card title attribute with an irrelevant value "Card 1" which could be better used for the heading of our text.

Here is an example where the title attribute inside the card tag is used to form a part of our message:

Notice here again the variation in the way that the emulators implement the code. The Nokia version, on the right, supports the <big> and <small> tag whereas the Ericsson emulator only supports a single font size.

There is a price to pay for the creative possibilities provided by the use of the <big> tag as it reduces the number of visible lines displayed.

This should be an important consideration and its use limited to cards with simple 2-line displays.

Document Type Definition

As WML is an XML application each WML document must start with a header tag declaring itself as a valid XML document using this tag:

<?xml version="1.0"?>

 All valid XML documents must contain a Document Type Definition.

The language rules that govern WML are contained in an XML document which is used by the phone to validate the WML content.

This XML document uses Standard General Markup Language (SGML) syntax to define all the permissible entities and structures that a WML document may contain.

For example this line permits the use of numbers 0-9 in a WML document:

<!ENTITY % number "NMTOKEN">

You do not need to understand the SGML code to write WAP content but it is useful to understand how the WML code is validated.

You do however need to include a header tag in every WML document to declare its Document Type Definition (DTD) by adding this code after the XML declaration given above:

<!DOCTYPE wml PUBLIC "-//WAPFORUM//DTD WML 1.1//EN" "http://www.wapforum.org/DTD/wml_1.1.xml">

The SGML public identifier declared with this line of code is "-//WAPFORUM//DTD WML 1.1//EN" and the URL is the location of the XML file containing the language rules.

The parser in the phone will then be able to refer to the rules in wml_1.1.xml in order to validate the content of that particular WML document.

In the event that the parser finds that the WML document content is valid the contents of the first card will be processed and displayed on the phone display screen.

Deck Navigation

This chapter illustrates how WML code enables the phone user to navigate around the deck moving between cards.

Covers

Chapter Three

Using Anchors

In order to create links to other addresses WML uses anchors in just the same way as the familiar <A HREF= syntax in HTML.

To make a simple link using the WML <A > element you need to include the destination address for the link. The target can be another deck or a card within the current deck:

```
<wml>
<card id="card1" title="Link Demo 1">
<p>
This is a
<a href="next.wml">link</a>
</p>
</card>
</wml>
```

The user can scroll to the link and select it using a soft key to load the target destination.

The deck above generates this display:

Text must be within <P> </P> elements and links can be inserted anywhere you would use text, except in an option.

The <A> element is useful for creating simple links and is the shortened version of the WML <ANCHOR> element.

The <ANCHOR> element has the extra ability to assign further tasks when the link is selected but you may only use one task with each anchor.

The link now works by assigning the task of loading the target to the <GO> element which can itself assign a further task. In this way the <ANCHOR> element has more flexibility than the simple <A> element:

```
<wml>
<card id="card1" title="Link Demo 2">
<p>This is a
<anchor>link
<go href="next.wml">
<!-- here is where we could assign a further task -->
</go>
</anchor>
</p>
</card>
</wml>
```

Elements that can be nested inside another element, like the <GO> element in this example, are referred to as "contained" elements.

In addition to the <GO> element the <ANCHOR> element can use the <PREV> element to locate to the previous address and the <REFRESH> element to reload the current URL.

The elements <GO> <PREV> <REFRESH> <NOOP> are referred to as "tasks" in WML.

The DO Element

The <DO> element is used to assign tasks to be performed on receipt of an interface action, generally when the user presses one of the soft keys on the phone.

This element must contain a TYPE= attribute to inform the phone how to carry out the action.

The most common use is to assign a confirmation to the left-hand soft key using an "accept" value or to assign backward navigation using a value of "prev", as in the following example using two cards:

Add a closing slash to the empty GO elements.

```
<wml>
<card id="card1" title="Card 1">
<do type="accept" label="Next">
<go href="#card2"/>
</do>
</card>
<card id="card2" title="Card 2">
<do type="prev" label="Back">
<go href="#card1"/>
</do>
</card>
</wml>
```

The cards are addressed using the # syntax just as in HTML and refer to the id value of each card. This is known as a fragment anchor.

<GO> elements in this example do not assign to further tasks and so are both considered as "empty" and have a trailing slash at the end of the tag to close the markup.

The <GO> element in Card 2 could have been replaced with a <PREV> element to return to Card 1.

Here is the interface generated by this example deck:

Notice how the Nokia emulator adds a default "Options" label over the left side of the screen while Ericsson prefer to leave more visible display.

In each case the left soft key will open a confirmation interface but these too are treated in a different manner. Nokia have assigned our "prev" task to the right soft key with a default "Back" label whereas Ericsson present both tasks in the Options list.

In each case the left softkey opens card 2 in the display but the user must press the right soft key with Nokia to action the "prev" task or scroll to the prev option and press the left soft key with Ericsson to return to card 1.

Adding Labels

The Nokia emulator will add default labels to the interface for navigation actions while Ericsson use the <DO> element's TYPE attribute value as a default label.

The way in which the user activates the DO element will vary on different phones depending upon the interface design.

To replace the default label with your own value simply add a LABEL attribute to each <DO> element as in this example that uses 3 cards:

```
<wml>

<card id="card1" title="Card 1">

<do type="accept" label="Go To Card 2">

<go href="#card2"/>

</do>

</card>

<card id="card2" title="Card 2">

<do type="prev" label="Go to Card 1">

<prev/>

</do>

<do type="accept" label="Go to Card 3">

<go href="#card3"/>

</do>

</card>

<card id="card3" title="Card 3">

<do type="prev" label="Back">

<prev/>

</do>

</card>

</wml>
```

Here is the Options interface generated after pressing the left soft key to navigate from card 2 to card 3 where the labels are displayed in the Ericsson Options menu:

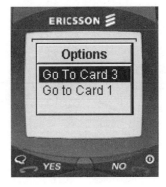

The Nokia emulator offers two versions of phone simulator which generate theses interfaces for the same navigation:

Use short text descriptions for DO labels.

The version on the right only displays the label for the DO "accept" type. The version on the left does not display any Options list but instead applies the DO label attribute values to the screen soft key labels. In this case the label text is too long to display correctly so it is best to use only short text labels to account for the variety of ways in which different phones may display the DO labels.

Browser Context

The browser context maintains a history record of URLs visited by the browser, just like a Web browser does.

The URLs are stored in a stack so that each time the user navigates to a new card the URL of that card is "pushed" on top of the stack.

Conversely when the user navigates backwards from a card the execution of the <PREV> element "pops" the current URL off the top of the stack thereby exposing the URL of the last card to be pushed onto the stack.

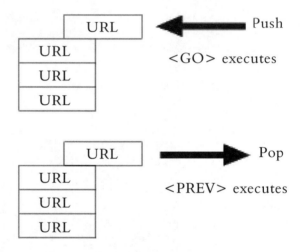

The browser history can be reset by emptying the stack.

To empty the stack WML provides a special attribute called "newcontext" which can be used in the <CARD> element.

Newcontext can only have a value of either true or false and if the attribute is not explicitly stated the value is assumed to be false.

When the newcontext attribute is set to "true", that card will be treated as though it was the first card in the deck and the user will be unable to navigate backwards from that card.

The browser history stack uses memory resources in the phone that may become exhausted with a large number of stored URLs.

The WML recommendation is for the phone makers to incorporate a history stack of at least 10 URLs. If this limit is exceeded the phone should delete the bottom URL in the stack to make room for the next addition.

This is an example using newcontext in Card 2:

```
<wml>
<card id= "card1" title= "Card 1">
<do type= "accept">
<go href= "#card2">
</do>
</card>
<card id= "card2" title= "Card 2" newcontext= "true">
<do type= "accept" label= "Back">
<prev/>
</do>
</card>
</wml>
```

Let's look at what is happening here:

- The URL of Card 1 is pushed onto the stack when the deck loads

- When the user navigates to Card 2 the newcontext instruction in Card 2 removes all the stack URLs

- So when the user tries to navigate backwards the softkey will not activate an action because the browser context is empty

Deck Templates

WML provides a way to save some code by use of the <TEMPLATE> element to apply common event tasks to each card in the deck.

The example below creates a deck with a home card plus three possible link destination cards. From each of the destination cards the user can navigate back to the home card using the <PREV> event task:

```
<wml>

<card id="home" title="Home Card" newcontext="true">

<p>

Go to <a href= "#link1">link 1</a><br/>

Go to <a href= "#link2">link 2</a>

</p>

</card>

<card id= "link1" title= "Link 1">

<do type= "prev" label= "Back"><prev/></do>

</card>

<card id= "link2" title= "Link 2">

<do type= "prev" label= "Back"><prev/></do>

</card>

<card id= "link2" title= "Link 2">

<do type= "prev" label= "Back"><prev/></do>

</card>

</wml>
```

This code is duplicating the <PREV> event binding in each card which is inefficient and can be better implemented using a deck template like the next example.

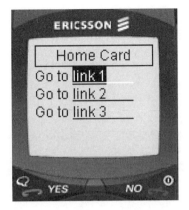 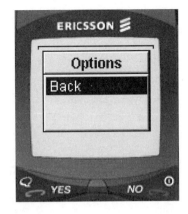

```
<wml>
<template>
<do type= "prev" label= "Back"><prev/></do>
</template>
<card id="home" title="Home Card" newcontext="true">
<p>
Go to <a href= "#link1">link 1</a><br/>
Go to <a href= "#link2">link 2</a><br/>
Go to <a href= "#link3">link 3</a>
</p>
</card>
<card id= "link1" title= "Link 1"></card>
<card id= "link2" title= "Link 2"></card>
<card id= "link3" title= "Link 3"></card>
</wml>
```

This code is more compact and the efficiency gain is even greater with larger numbers of cards in the deck.

Task Override

Tasks that have been bound to events at deck level using the <TEMPLATE> element may be overridden at card level.

The card level task will override the template event binding:

1 If the card level task specifies the same event

2 If the card level <ONEVENT> element has the same type

3 If the card level <DO> element has the same name

```
<wml>
<template>
<do type="prev" label="Back"><prev/></do>
</template>
<card id="home" title="Home Card" newcontext="true">
<p>
Go to <a href= "#link1">link 1</a><br/>
Go to <a href= "#link2">link 2</a><br/>
Go to <a href= "#link3">link 3</a></p>
</card>
<card id= "link1" title= "Link 1"></card>
<card id= "link2" title= "Link 2">
<do type= "prev"><noop/></do>
</card>
<card id= "link3" title= "Link 3">
<do type= "prev" label= "Go Home"><prev/></do>
</card>
</wml>
```

In this example the <TEMPLATE> event binding is overridden at card level in cards "Link 2" and "Link 3".

Link 1 still uses the default task in the template. Link 2 uses the WML task <NOOP>to specify a no-operation task should be bound to the <PREV> event.

This effectively removes the event from the card completely.

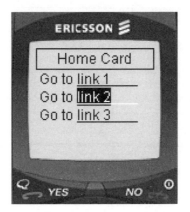 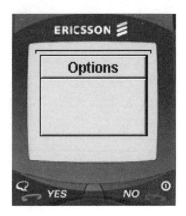

Link 3 replaces the template "Back" label with its own.

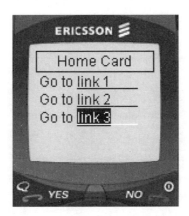 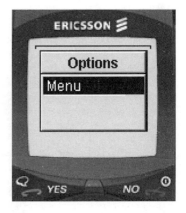

In this way the template can efficiently bind events to tasks as defaults where only cards having overrides need to have additional code.

Special Characters

WML supports the use of character entities, in the same way that HTML does, to allow the use of characters which have a special meaning within the markup language itself.

The character entities may be specified either by name or by numeric reference, so you can include an ampersand, for example, using either **&** or **&**

Character entities referenced in numeric form will always display the same logical characters as they refer to the Unicode character rather than any document encoded character set.

Character	Name Reference	Numeric Reference
Ampersand	&	&
Apostrophe	'	'
Quotation Mark	"	"
Less Than	<	<
Greater Than	>	>
Nonbreaking Space		
Soft Hyphen	­	­

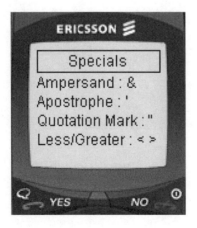

Options and Built-In Events

This chapter introduces Options menus and also explains the intrinsic events that are part of WML. You will learn how to create options from which the user may select and how to use WML-intrinsic events within elements.

Covers

Chapter Four

Option Menus

WML follows the syntax used in HTML to create Option menus using the familiar <SELECT> element to create the list and the <OPTION> element for each list item.

This example creates an Option menu with three choices:

```
<wml>
<card id= "card1" title= "Color Options">
<p>Choose a color
<select name= "colormenu">
<option value= "red">Red</option>
<option value= "green">Green</option>
<option value= "blue">Blue</option>
</select>
</p>
</card>
</wml>
```

The <OPTION> elements are contained within the <SELECT> element and unlike HTML they must include the closing tags. Notice that the entire <SELECT> element is itself contained within the <P> element.

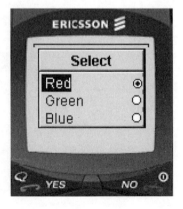

By default the user can only select one option but multiple selections can be allowed by setting the "multiple" attribute to "true" in the <SELECT> element.

The "title" attribute for the <SELECT> element may be used to set the displayed text to other than the default value.

The index values do not start at 0 as you might expect.

The option to be displayed by default is the first option in the list but may be set using the "ivalue" attribute of the <SELECT> element. This is an index value of the list of options which starts at "1" for the first element:

```
<wml>

<card id= "card1" title= "Color Options"><p>

<select name= "colormenu" title= "Choose:"
multiple="true" ivalue="2">

<option value= "red">Red</option>

<option value= "green">Green</option>

<option value= "blue">Blue</option>

</select></p>

</card>

</wml>
```

Use the "title" attributes to keep the code efficient.

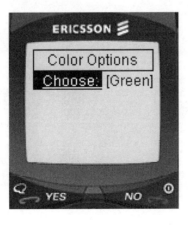

Option Groups

WML provides a special <OPTGROUP> element to group together associated options in order to provide the user with a top tier of selections:

```
<wml>
<card id= "card1" title= "Main Menu">
<p><select name= "menu">
<optgroup title= "color">
<option value= "red">Red</option>
<option value= "green">Green</option>
<option value= "blue">Blue</option>
</optgroup>
<optgroup title= "size">
<option value= "small">Small</option>
<option value= "medium">Medium</option>
<option value= "large">Large</option>
</optgroup>
<optgroup title= "shape">
<option value= "square">Square</option>
<option value= "circle">Circle</option>
<option value= "triangle">Triangle</option>
</optgroup>
</select>
</p>
</card>
</wml>
```

This example presents three Option groups for selection.

First the user may scroll to the Option group from which they wish to select. Pressing the left-hand soft key will then create the selected Option group options from which the final selection can be made.

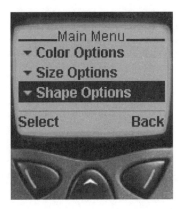

The way in which the phone may implement the Option groups in the interface can vary.

The illustration above shows the Nokia emulator correctly implementing the code whereas the Ericsson emulator I was using does not yet support Option groups and simply places all the options together in one selection list. Check the release notes with the emulator for unsupported items.

Onpick

The onpick event occurs each time a user selects an option. The onpick attribute of the <OPTION> element can be used to go to the URL specified with the onpick attribute value.

In this example the phone will go to the card or deck specified within the chosen option's onpick attribute:

```
<!-- file: red.wml -->

<wml>

<card id= "menu" title= "Menu">

<p><select name= "colors">

<option value= "red" onpick= "#redcard">Red</option>

<option value= "blue" onpick= "blue.wml#bluecard">

Blue</option>

</select><p>

</card>

<card id= "redcard" title= "This is the Red Card">

</card>

</wml>
```

```
<!-- file: blue.wml -->

<wml>

<card id="card1" title="First Card in this Deck">

</card>

<card id="bluecard" title="This is the Blue Card">

</card>

</wml>
```

The Options soft key produces the available options from which the user may select and the "onpick" task will go to the appropriate URL for the selected option.

The URL for the Red option is another card within the same deck but the URL for the Blue option is a card located in another deck.

The method of addressing the card for the Blue option uses the WML filename followed by the id value of the card.

If the card is not expressly addressed then the phone would just display the first card in the deck in the same way that the first card is displayed by default when any deck opens.

Onenterforward

The <ONEVENT> element in WML is used to bind a task to a built-in event and is especially useful for actioning tasks during navigation using the <GO> element.

This example relocates the phone to card 3 when card 2 is entered forward but will still display card 2 when the user navigates backward from card 3:

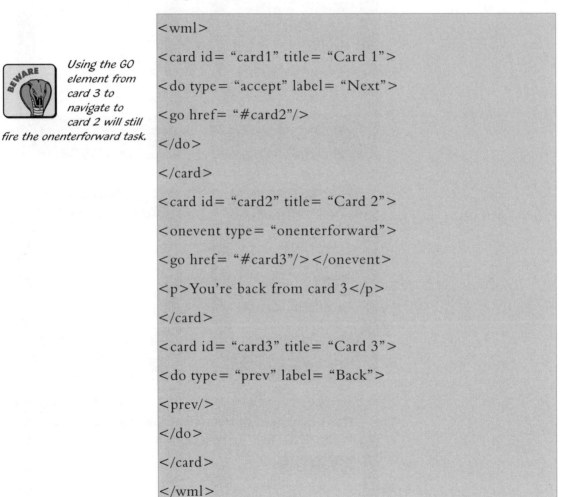

```
<wml>

<card id= "card1" title= "Card 1">

<do type= "accept" label= "Next">

<go href= "#card2"/>

</do>

</card>

<card id= "card2" title= "Card 2">

<onevent type= "onenterforward">

<go href= "#card3"/></onevent>

<p>You're back from card 3</p>

</card>

<card id= "card3" title= "Card 3">

<do type= "prev" label= "Back">

<prev/>

</do>

</card>

</wml>
```

The user may momentarily see the card having the onenterforward event before the task is actioned in the same way that Web pages containing relocation scripts will display briefly before the script is actioned.

Onenterbackward

The <ONEVENT> element can be used to bind tasks to the <PREV> element when the user performs backward navigation.

Here Card 1 displays normally when entered forward but relocates to Card 3 if the user navigates back from Card 2:

```
<wml>

<card id= "card1" title= "Card 1">

<onevent type= "onenterbackward">

<go href= "#card3"/></onevent>

<p><a href= "#card2">Go to card 2</a></p>

</card>

<card id= "card2" title= "Card 2">

<do type= "prev" label= "Back"><prev/></do>

</card>

<card id= "card3" title= "Card 3">

<p>You're back from Card 2</p>

</card>

</wml>
```

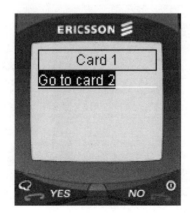
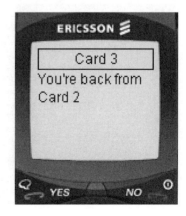

Ontimer

WML provides a built-in timer using the <ONTIMER> event that can be used to relocate to a specified URL after the timer expires.

An alternative means of navigating to the target URL should always be provided in case the timer fails.

The example displays a "splash screen" for 3 seconds before going on to the menu that can also be reached by the <DO> event associated with the soft key:

The timer value is expressed in tenths of a second instead of the usual millisecond values used by other scripting languages.

```
<wml>
<card id="card1" ontimer="#card2" title="Splash">
<timer value= "30"/>
<do type= "accept" label= "Next">
<go href= "#card2"/>
</do>
<p align= "center"><b>Welcome!</b></p></card>
<card id= "card2" title= "Menu">
<p>Here by Timer or<br/>Here by Soft key</p>
</card>
</wml>
```

Variables in WML

This chapter deals with the use of variable Values in WML. You will learn how variables can be used in writing WML content and how their values can be set and changed.

Covers

Chapter Five

Variables in Content

WML supports the use of variables directly within text content where the value of the variable will be substituted into the flow of text.

Always use lowercase only for naming variables to avoid problems with capitalisation errors.

Variable values may also be used as option values and with href to provide a link URL.

When naming variables the first character may only be a letter or an underscore. All other characters must only be letters, underscores or digits.

Variable names are case sensitive so variables named "The_Var", "the_var" and "THE_VAR" would be treated as three different variables.

The placing of variable names inside brackets is highly recommended.

A variable reference uses a dollar sign ($) followed by the name given to the variable. So a variable named "the_var" would be referred to in the WML code as "$the_var" or the name can be enclosed in brackets to become "$(the_var)".

Do not enter the quote marks.

To use an actual dollar sign inside the variable value it must be escaped using another dollar sign. So that a value of "$$10" would appear when substituted into text as "$10".

When a variable is substituted the format of the variable value may be converted by adding a conversion type to the bracketed variable name. This conversion can be used to specify if the format should be escaped, unescaped or if there should be no escape at all.

The conversion to escape any non-alphanumeric characters uses the syntax "$(the_var:escape)" or simply "$(the_var:e)".

To convert the value unescaping any non-alphanumeric characters uses just "$(the_var:unesc)" while no escape at all can be specified using either "$(the_var:noesc)" or more simply just "$(the_var:N)".

If no conversion is expressly specified the format will undergo automatic escape conversion when the variable is substituting attributes with onenterbackward, onenterforward, src and href.

Setting Value by Refresh

The WML <SETVAR> element is used to set the variables value by association with the execution of a task.

The WML <REFRESH> task is commonly used in this way.

In the following example, the <DO> element binds the <REFRESH> task in order to use <SETVAR>:

```
<wml>
<card id= "card1" title= "Variables">
<do type= "accept" label= "Setvar">
<refresh>
<setvar name= "var" value= "First Variable"/>
</refresh>
</do>
<p>My $(var)</p>
</card>
</wml>
```

Until the value of the variable is set it is simply ignored when the WML code is parsed. When the user sets the value the screen is refreshed and the value is displayed.

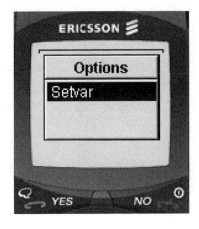
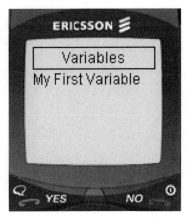

Setting Value by Navigation

The parser in the phone will only read the variable values after completing the elements and entities in the deck. This means that variables cannot be initialised when a deck first loads but must be set using events within the browser context.

This example overcomes the difficulty by immediately refreshing the deck after it loads.

The onenterforward event binds the WML <REFRESH> task and the <SETVAR> element:

```
<wml>

<card id= "card1" title= "Variables">

<onevent type= "onenterforward">

<refresh>

<setvar name= "var" value= "Welcome Variable"/>

</refresh>

</onevent>

<p>$(var)</p>

</card>

</wml>
```

In the previous example the variable value will be set each time the user navigates to this card. This method of setting variables can be used with both the onenterforward and the onenterbackward event in any card.

In the example below the variable is set when the user enters Card 1 then is reset when the user navigates back to Card 1:

```
<wml>
<card id= "card1" title= "Card 1">
<onevent type= "onenterforward"><refresh>
<setvar name= "var" value= "First Value"/>
</refresh></onevent>
<onevent type= "onenterbackward"><refresh>
<setvar name= "var" value= "Second Value"/>
</refresh></onevent>
<p>$(var)<br><a href= "card2">NEXT</a></p>
</card>
<card id= "card2" title= "Card 2"></card>
</wml>
```

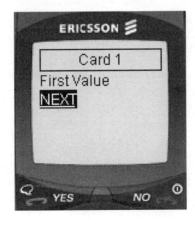
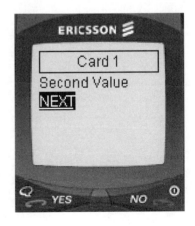

Setting Value by Selection

The use of the soft key enables the user to change the value of the variable in this example.

When the card is first loaded the onenterforward event uses the WML <REFRESH> element to set the variable value. When the user selects a soft key option the <REFRESH> task applies the new value to the display:

```
<wml>
<card id= "card1" title= "Set Value">
<onevent type= "onenterforward">
<refresh><setvar name= "color" value= "Red"/>
</refresh>
</onevent>
<do type= "accept" name= "set_blue" label= "Set Blue">
<refresh>
<setvar name= "color" value= "Blue"/>
</refresh>
</do>
<do type= "accept" name= "set_green"
label= "Set Green">
<refresh>
<setvar name= "color" value="Green"/>
</refresh>
</do>
<p>Color is $(color)</p>
</card>
</wml>
```

Setting Value by Input

A variable may be declared and initialised using the WML <INPUT> element to have the user set the variable value.

The <INPUT> element can appear anywhere in normal text but may be implemented in different ways on different phones.

In the example below notice that the Nokia emulator does not display the title value to identify the input.

The user presses a soft key to reach the input interface then enters the required data using the alpha values marked upon the keypad.

When the entry is confirmed by a further press of a soft key the variable value is set to the entered data value:

```
<wml>
<card id= "card1" title= "Set Value">
<p>
<input type= "text" name= "var" title= "Name: "/>
</p>
</card>
</wml>
```

It is much more difficult to enter text input than to select an option, so give options where possible.

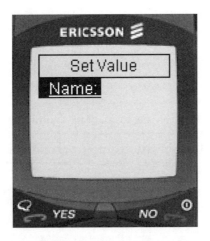

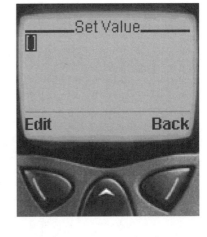

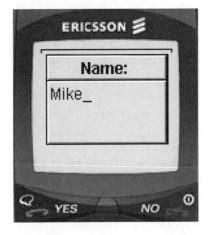

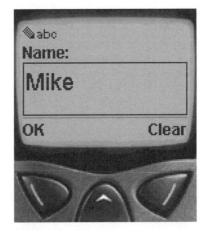

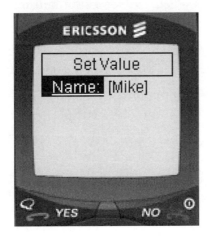

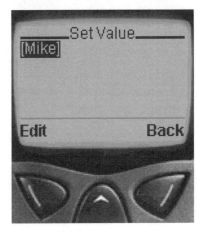

Input Formats

The <INPUT> element may contain the "format" attribute to specify the permissible format for entries by the user.

The table below details the available restrictions:

A	All uppercase characters that are non-numeric only
a	All lowercase characters that are non-numeric only
N	All numeric characters only
X	All uppercase characters only
x	All lowercase characters only
M	All characters but they may be displayed in uppercase
m	All characters but they may be displayed in lowercase

The permissible length of the input may be specified by prefixing any format with a limiting number, for example format="4N" specifies that the input must be 4 numbers.

When a numeric-only format is specified the keypad will normally just enter numbers and the alpha values will only display when the format is set to non-numeric formats.

An asterisk may be used to specify unlimited length of input so format="*X" allows unlimited uppercase characters.

Although the WML <INPUT> element can accept a "size" and a "maxlength" attribute like HTML, it is advisable to use the "format" attribute to restrict input size.

It is possible to allow the user to input an empty value by adding the "emptyok" attribute with a value of "true".

This example permits 4 numbers or an empty value:

```
<input name="var" emptyok="true" format="4N"/>
```

Password Input

In order to preserve the security of passwords on entry the <INPUT> element may specify a "type" attribute with a value of "password" in place of the default text type.

The input value is stored in the usual manner but the characters are replaced with an asterisk in the display.

The example below permits the entry of any characters into a password whose length must be 5 characters:

This is low-level security intended only to protect passwords from casual view on entry.

```
<wml>

<card id= "card1" title= "Enter Password">

<p>

<input name= "var" type= "password"

title= "Password" format= "5m"/>

</p>

</card>

</wml>
```

Fieldsets

The WML <FIELDSET> element provides a way in which content layout may be influenced by grouping together associated text and fields.

This example groups name and data into fieldsets but the layout may choose not to use the fieldset information:

```
<wml>
<card id= "card1" title= "User Info">
<p><fieldset title= "username">
<input name="fname" title="FirstName" format="*A"/>
<input name="lname" title="LastName" format="*A"/>
</fieldset>
<fieldset title="userdata">
<input name= "age" title= "Age" format= "2N"/>
<select name= "sex"><option title="Male" value="M"/>
<option title= "Female" value= "F"/></select>
</fieldset></p>
</card>
</wml>
```

The particular phone may use the fieldset information to create a layout.

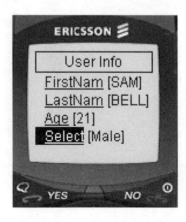

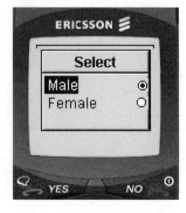

Tables and Images

This chapter describes how to display images and tables. You will learn about how to create images in the Wireless Bitmap (WBMP) format and discover how to use table layouts to control the phone display.

Covers

Chapter Six

Tables

The use of tables in WML is a much simplified version of the way that tables can be used in HTML. The <TABLE> element is used along with the <TR> and <TD> elements to define the way that the phone should display rows and columns.

Tables may not be nested and the phone may interpret the layout only loosely as the width and height of table cells may not be specified with attributes.

The <TABLE> element must always contain a "columns" attribute to determine the exact number of columns needed:

```
<wml>
<card id= "card1" title= "Tables">
<p><table columns= "3">
<tr>
<td><a href= "#card2">
<img src= "btn1.wbmp" alt= "btn1"/></a></td>
<td><a href= "#card3">
<img src= "btn2.wbmp" alt= "btn2"/></a></td>
<td><a href= "#card4">
<img src= "btn3.wbmp" alt= "btn3"/></a></td>
</tr>
</table>
</p></card>
<card id= "card2" title= "Card 2"></card>
<card id= "card3" title= "Card 3"></card>
<card id= "card4" title= "Card 4"></card>
</wml>
```

The example uses a table to control the layout of images that are links to other cards within the deck.

The Nokia emulator makes the table display far more compactly by having much less padding around the cell data.

Cells containing images may influence the cell size by the use of the <IMG> attributes "vspace" and "hspace" but this is dependent upon the implementation by the phone:

```
<td>
<img src="i.wbmp" vspace="7" hspace="25" alt="info"/>
</td>
```

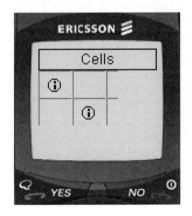 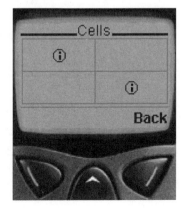

Creating Images

WBMP is the special graphic format used by WML to display images on the phone screen as efficiently as possible.

It is a simple 2-bit format displaying only black-and-white images in order to minimize the amount of byte code needed to download images to the phone.

WAP does not support other formats such as GIF and JPG.

The Nokia emulator has an integral WBMP editor which will allow the author to create images in WBMP format and permits the import of images in GIF and JPG formats for conversion to WBMP. Whilst the Nokia image editor does produce WBMP images it is easier to use a graphics package with which you are more familiar.

A free plug-in is available (from http://www.rcp.co.uk) to create and edit WBMP files in these popular graphics applications: Adobe Photoshop and Paint Shop Pro.

The plug-in when used with Photoshop always saves WBMP images with a file extension .WBM instead of the true extension name .WBMP. This means that WBMP images created in this way have to be renamed.

To create a new WBMP image with Photoshop you need to open a new file of type "Bitmap" to be sure that the WBMP format will appear as a "Save As" format option.

Converting a colour GIF image in Photoshop first requires selecting Grayscale mode to discard the colour information, then Bitmap mode to convert the file type. Some interesting method options are presented at this point to determine how the image may appear.

This file extension problem does not arise when using the plug-in with Paint Shop Pro as the WBMP images are saved with the correct extension. Converting colour GIF images is simply a matter of opening the GIF file and then saving it as a WBMP file.

Displaying Images

The WML <IMG> element is used to display images and the "alt" attribute is mandatory to specify text to be displayed in the event that the image is not loaded:

```
<wml>
<card id= "card1" title= "Hello World">
<p align= "center">
<img src= "sphere.wbmp" alt= "sphere"/><br/>
<b>SYSTEME</b>
</p> </card> </wml>
```

Images as Links

Images can be used as links in the same way as with HTML although the linking image will always have a border.

The image in this example is a link to another card that uses the same image in a link to return to Card 1:

```
<wml>

<card id= "card1" title= "Hello World">

<p align= "center">

<a href= "#card2">

<img src= "eye.wbmp" alt= "eye"/></a>

</p>

</card>

<card id= "card2" title= "Card 2">

<p align= "center"><a href= "#card1">

<img src= "eye.wbmp" alt= "eye"/></a>

</p>

</card>

</wml>
```

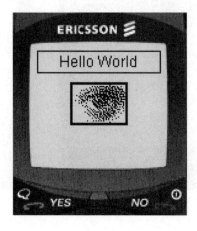 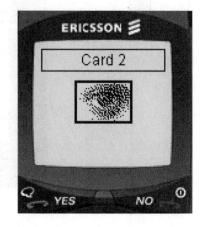

Aligning Images

The WML <IMG> element may contain an "align" attribute to position the image vertically within the context of the current flow of text.

The possible values for "align" position the image vertically relative to the current text line with possible values of "top", "middle" or "bottom":

```
<wml>

<card id= "card1" title= "Image Align">

<p>

The <img align= "top" src= "key.wbmp" width= "6"
height= "6" alt= "key"/> top <br/>

The <img align= "middle" src= "key.wbmp" width= "6"
height= "6" alt= "key"/> middle <br/>

The <img align= "bottom" src= "key.wbmp" width= "6"
height= "6" alt= "key"/> bottom

</p>

</card>

</wml>
```

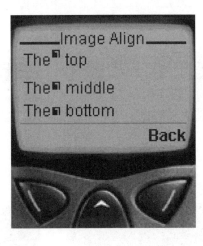

Spacing Images

Images may be used as links but the way that the phone may layout the images can vary, as in this example. The Nokia emulator displays the link images on the same line but Ericsson centres the links and adds vertical spacing:

```
<wml>

<card id= "card1" title= "Navigation Bar">

<p>

<a href= "#card2"><img src= "btn1.wbmp" alt= "btn1"
vspace= "2" hspace= "2"/></a>

<a href= "#card3"><img src= "btn2.wbmp" alt= "btn2"
vspace= "2" hspace= "2"/></a>

<a href= "#card4"><img src= "btn3.wbmp" alt= "btn3"
vspace= "2" hspace= "2"/></a>

</p>

</card>

<card id= "card2" title= "Card 2"></card>

<card id= "card3" title= "Card 3"></card>

<card id= "card4" title= "Card 4"></card>

</wml>
```

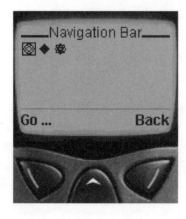

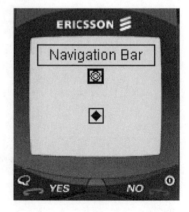

Environment and Security

This chapter describes how to set up a WAP environment on a PC system and how WML provides security. You will learn how to install a free Web server and configure it for the WAP environment to enable local application tests.

Covers

Chapter Seven

Xitami Web Server

The Xitami Web server is a freeware application that is supplied bundled along with the Ericsson WapIDE.

It is produced by the iMatix Corporation and is available for free download from their website at http://www.imatix.com.

Xitami can be used to easily simulate a WAP environment on a local PC system in order to test WAP applications while not connected to the Internet.

Install Xitami to the default location of C:\Xitami.

The installer provides the option to have Xitami added to the Windows Startup group or you may manually start Xitami when it is needed for testing.

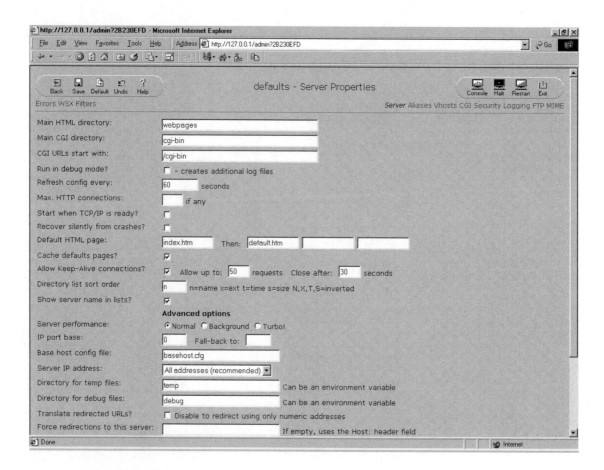

Configuring MIME Types

The Xitami server installs ready to run without any further configuration but it is necessary to add the WAP MIME types to the server's vocabulary so that it will recognise the WAP file formats.

To configure Xitami with the WAP MIME types the configuration file "C:\Xitami\xitami.cfg" can be opened in any text editor such as Notepad.

The list of MIME types that are already configured can be found toward the end of the file and the WAP types below need to be added into that list:

```
# WAP MIME types

wml=text/vnd.wap.wml

wmls=text/vnd.wap.wmlscript

wmlc=text/vnd.wap/wmlc

wmlsc=text/vnd.wap.wmlscriptc

wbmp=image/vnd.wap.wbmp
```

The WAP file formats will now be recognised and WAP applications can be tested from Xitami.

Xitami has a directory folder at C:\Xitami\webpages where all WML files should be deposited for testing.

Any local WAP browser can access the WML files located on the Xitami server using HTTP and the domain "localhost".

For example, to load a file called "test.wml", first start Xitami, then use the URL "http://localhost/test.wml":

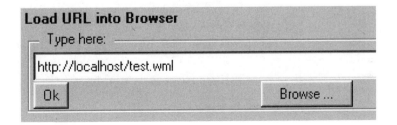

Server-Side Scripting

The Ericsson WapIDE includes support for server-side scripts with the inclusion of Perl for the Windows platform so that CGI scripts can be tested in the WAP environment.

Perl is also available for free download for installation under Windows from http://www.ActiveState.com and includes excellent documentation.

Install Perl to the default location of C:\Perl.

The path line SET PATH=C:\PERL\BIN; will be added to the autoexec.bat file on the system during installation.

The Xitami Web server has a directory called "cgi-bin" where all CGI scripts should be placed in order to be accessible.

The creation of Perl scripts is a separate topic outside the parameters of this book. It is worth noting however that the standard header, or so-called "shebang" line that is used in Perl scripts, is generally "#!/usr/local/bin/perl". This should be replaced in the test environment with "#!c:/perl/bin/perl" so that the Perl interpreter can be located.

A Perl CGI script called "test.pl" in the WAP test environment could be addressed using this URL reference: "http://localhost/cgi-bin/test.pl":

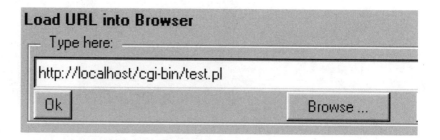

Ericsson also bundle support for server-side scripting using the Tool Control Language TCL/TK for which more information is available at http://www.tclconsortium.org.

Dynamic Content

The Ericsson WapIDE includes a custom Perl library to facilitate the dynamic creation of WML content.

To use the library place the file "wmllib.pl" in the Web-server script directory at "C:/Xitami/cgi-bin" together with support files "config.pl" and "demoutils.pl". Then edit the shebang and path in each file to the correct Perl location.

This example generates a simple line of text.

```
#!c:/perl/bin/perl

require 'wmllib.pl';

$attributes{'id'} = "card1";

$attributes{'class'} = "cgitest";

$content = &Card(&P("Generated by CGI",\%attributes));

$attributes{'id'} = "deck1";

print &Deck($content,\%attributes);
```

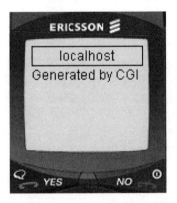 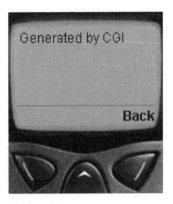

The Nokia WAP Toolkit contains an example to create dynamic WML content using Java but requires the installation of Sun's XML library.

This is available for free download from Sun's website at http://developer.java.sun.com/developer/products/xml.

Postfield

The WML <POSTFIELD> element is used to send "name=value" pairs back to the Web server when the phone requests a URL.

This example sends a single data pair to the Web server using the HTTP POST method which the CGI script uses:

```
<wml><card id= "card1" title= "Submit Data"><p>
<anchor>Send Username
<go method= "post"
href= "http://localhost/cgi-bin/usr.pl">
<postfield name= "User" value= "Mike"/>
</go></anchor></p></card></wml>
```

```
#!c:/Perl/bin/perl
require 'demoutils.pl';
require 'wmllib.pl';
%cgivars = &ParseCGIVars();
$user=$cgivars{"User"};
$content = &Card(&P("User is $user"));
print &Deck($content);
```

Access Security

The WML <ACCESS> element may be used only once in any deck to specify which other decks may have access to this deck and is contained within the <HEAD> element.

If the <ACCESS> element is not specified then the deck may be accessed by any card in any deck.

The "domain" and "path" attributes are used to determine which other decks can access the current deck.

As the user navigates from deck to deck the phone performs access control checks with each move. If a deck contains an <ACCESS> element then the URL of the referring deck must match the domain and path specified by the access controls. The phone will first check that the domain part of the URL is correct then check that the path part of the URL matches.

This example requires the referrer to be in the "localhost" domain within a directory called "x":

```
<head><access domain="localhost" path="/x"/></head>
```

Failure to comply with the access control specifications causes an error message to appear in the phone advising the user that access is denied to that deck:

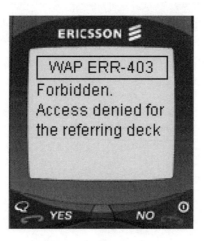

Meta Information

The WML <META> element may be used only once in any deck to specify generic data relating to the deck and is contained within the <HEAD> element.

The meta information is specified inside the <META> element using property names and values.

A "content" attribute is mandatory to describe the property value as the nature of the meta information.

The "name" attribute may be used to specify the name of the property but meta information using this attribute will not be sent to the phone by the network servers.

Meta information may be sent to the phone as a HTTP header by using the attribute "http-equiv" in place of the "name" attribute.

A common use could be to advise the phone of the character set used in the WML deck as in this example:

```
<head>
<meta content= "charset"
http-equiv= "character-set=UTF-8"/>
</head>
```

A further attribute of "forua" may be used to signify that the meta information should be sent to the phone when set with a value of "true".

WML also provides an attribute called "scheme" which may be used inside the <META> element to specify a value to determine how the property should be interpreted.

Adding Functionality

This chapter introduces the Wireless Markup Language Script (WMLScript) and illustrates its use in the WAP environment. You will learn about WMLScript variables and discover how WMLScript functions are called.

Covers

Chapter Eight

Introducing WMLScript

WMLScript is the part of Wireless Application Protocol that can be used to add functionality to WML decks and cards.

The language is similar to the familiar Javascript language that is used to add functionality to HTML documents.

WMLScript is a modified version of the ECMAScript language that has had some of the advanced features removed in order to make it smaller and easier to compile into byte code.

The intention is to reduce the download weight when the WAP gateway sends a WMLScript to the phone. This is made even more effective by the support of libraries which are pre-installed on the phone to further reduce the amount of code needing to be downloaded.

WMLScript has been designed to add capabilities to static WML content allowing manipulation of data by the script at local level inside the phone.

The script is stored as a text format file with the extension .WMLS on the Web server. The file is compiled by the WAP gateway then sent to the phone, in the same manner as WML content.

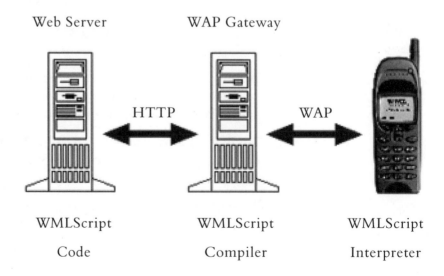

Web Server	WAP Gateway	
WMLScript	WMLScript	WMLScript
Code	Compiler	Interpreter

The Script Interpreter

The binary format of the code is interpreted in the phone by the WMLScript interpreter.

The WMLScript interpreter is used when the user performs an operation in the interface that calls a WMLScript function. The interpreter then executes the instructions in the function and returns the result to the interface.

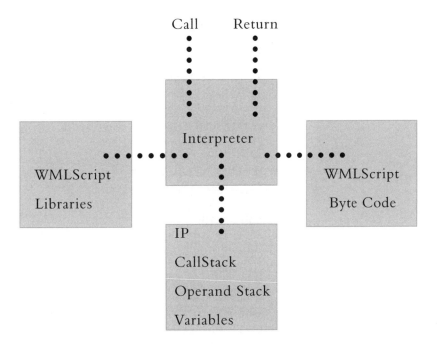

The interpreter uses an Instruction Pointer (IP) to keep track of the current instruction and maintains the record of the value of Variables in the script.

The WMLScript function can call other functions and their addresses are stored in their Call Stack whereas the Operand Stack is used to perform evaluation of arguments.

This provides functionality not present in WML including input validation, dialog messages, mathematical operations and string manipulation.

Declaring Variables

A variable in WMLScript is used to store a piece of data for use by the script and consists of a name and value pair.

The variable must be declared in the script before it can be used and needs only the keyword "var" to declare the name to be valid. For example:

```
var a;
```

declares a variable named "a" using the var keyword.

(The end semicolon is required to terminate all statements.)

In this example the variable name is declared without stating an initial value.

All uninitialised variables are given by default an empty string value (" ").

The next example declares a variable and immediately initializes it with a value:

```
var n=1;
```

The initialized value is an integer type with a value of 1.

The type of variable need not be declared as WMLScript is a weakly-typed language where any variable can contain any type of variable data. The parser will perform automatic data conversion to the data type appropriate for the context.

Types of variable data supported by WMLScript are "boolean", "integer", "float", "string" and "invalid" as seen in the examples below:

Comments can be single-line (using "//" as seen here) or multi-line (starting "/*" & ending "*/").

```
var flag=true;       // boolean

var int=20;          // integer

var flt=9.99;        // float

var str="Hello";     // string

var except=invalid;  // invalid
```

Using Variables

All variables in WMLScript must be declared inside a function and will only exist until the function ends. These are termed "local" variables as they exist locally within a function.

WMLScript does not support the use of global variables that are accessible to many functions, due to the limited memory resources available inside the phone.

The example below illustrates the correct declaration of a variable inside a function with an initial string value:

 Variable names in WMLScript are case-sensitive so be sure to use the correct capitalisation.

```
function get_user(){

var user= "Mike";

return user;

}
```

When called the function returns the variable value.

The next example illustrates some errors with variables:

```
var the_user; // declared outside a function

function get_user(){

user= "Mike"; // used before declaration - no var keyword

var newuser= "Fred";

return var newuser; // redeclaration - already declared var

}
```

As WMLScript variables are always used inside a function they are clearly different to the variables in WML and so do not become confused.

Although global variables are not permitted in WMLScript the variable and its value can be passed from function to function by including the variable as a function argument.

Declaring Functions

The active part of WMLScript is contained within functions.

A function is declared using the "function" keyword followed by the name being given to that function.

The function name is followed by a pair of brackets which may contain optional parameters, or arguments, to be used by the function.

Finally comes the block statement that is executed when the function is called, contained within parentheses.

The example below has an initial test value passed as an argument for evaluation.

The function will return a variable value dependant upon the result of the test value evaluation:

To avoid capitalisation problems, never use upper-case characters when naming variables or functions.

```
function first(the_value){

var result;

if(the_value < 100) result= "Below 100";

if(the_value > 100) result= "Above 100";

return result;

}
```

Functions cannot be nested and must bear a unique name within that script to avoid confusion in the parser.

The function may take more than one argument but the number of arguments must be matched when the function is called. For instance, calling the example below with "run(1,2)" will cause an error:

```
function run(a,b,c)
```

The function declares 3 arguments should be passed when calling this function. So "run(1,2,3)" will correctly call the function and pass the integer values 1,2,3 as the argument parameters for processing by the function.

Using Functions

In practice the WMLScript functions will normally always pass at least one argument as the value to be processed by the function. The example below shows how an initial value passed to the first function can be passed to other functions for manipulation before the first function returns the result:

Local functions may be called within the same file even before the function has been declared.

```
function first(the_value){

var result;

if(the_value < 100)result=second(the_value);

if(the_value > 100)result=third(the_value);

return result;

}

function second(the_value){

if(the_value < 50)return "Below 50";

if(the_value > 50)return "Above 50 & Below 100";

}

function third(val){

if(val < 150)return "Above 100 & Below 150";

if(val > 150)return "Above 150";

}
```

Keep the same names throughout to make the code more user-friendly and use short, meaningful names.

The name of the argument is abbreviated in the third function but works just as well because the name is only used locally inside that function and is only used to reference the value that has been passed as the argument.

This example makes use of local function calls as the functions are all located within the same file.

The first function can be called just by using its name and passing an argument value for manipulation. The call "first(25)" would return "Below 50" in this case.

External Accessibility

Functions within a WMLScript file (.WMLS) will by default be only available for call locally inside the file unless they are declared using the "extern" keyword.

In this example the second function is declared using the "extern" keyword and so it may be called from outside the WMLScript file whereas the first and third functions cannot:

```
function first(the_value){

var result;

if(the_value < 100)result=second(the_value);

if(the_value > 100)result=third(the_value);

return result;

}

extern function second(the_value){

if(the_value < 50)return "Below 50";

if(the_value > 50)return "Above 50";

}

function third(val){

if(val < 150)return "Above 100 & Below 150";

if(val > 150)return "Above 150";

}
```

It is necessary to ensure that at least one of the functions within a WMLScript file is externally available (and thus useful) so that the function can be called from a WML deck or another WMLScript file.

External Calls

To call a function from outside the local WMLScript file the function call must be prefixed with the remote file location.

In the example a header instruction called a "pragma" gives a local name to the location of the remote file.

The second function can then be called from its remote location using the location name and function name separated by a hash mark:

```
// filename : first.wmls

use url remote "http://localhost/second.wmls";

extern function first(the_value){

var result;

if(the_value < 100)result=remote#second(the_value);

if(the_value > 100)result=third(the_value);

return result;

}

function third(val){

if(val < 150)return "Above 100 & Below 150";

if(val > 150)return "Above 150";

}
```

The remote file contains the second function:

```
// filename : second.wmls

extern function second(the_value){

if(the_value < 50)return "Below 50";

if(the_value > 50)return "Above 50";

}
```

Library Calls

Library function calls are made to one of the standard WMLScript libraries that are built-in to the phone as part of the WAP standard.

A library function may be called simply using the name of the library followed by a dot (.) and the name of the function itself.

All WMLScript libraries are detailed fully later in this book.

The example below uses one of these libraries named "WMLBrowser" which has an intrinsic function "setVar()".

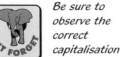

The setVar() function takes two arguments to return a name and value that may be applied to a WML variable.

In the example setVar() is applying a value of "Flamingo" to a variable named "var".

Another of the functions in the WMLBrowser library is used to refresh the phone display after the variable value has been updated so that the new value will appear:

```
extern function amend(){

WMLBrowser.setVar( "var", "Flamingo");

WMLBrowser.refresh();

}
```

The WML file on the facing page uses the refresh task with the onenterforward event to declare the variable named "var" and allocate an initial value to it of "Buffalo".

When the user presses the YES soft key to run the script the variable value is changed to "Flamingo" and the phone display refreshes to display this new value.

Trying this example with the Xitami Web server in a test environment requires that files script1.wml and script1.wmls be placed in the location C:\Xitami\Webpages, then with Xitami running load http://localhost/script1.wml to start.

The example code in this book usually omits the required headers to save space.

Use a "$" to escape the second "$" in order to display a dollar sign.

```xml
<?xml version="1.0"?>

<!DOCTYPE wml PUBLIC "-//WAPFORUM//DTD WML
1.1//EN" "http://www.wapforum.org/DTD/wml_1.1.xml">

<wml>

<card id="card1" title="First Script">

<onevent type="onenterforward">

<refresh>

<setvar name="var" value="Buffalo"/>

</refresh>

</onevent>

<p>

$$var is $var<br/>

Press YES to run script

<do type="accept">

<go href="script1.wmls#amend()"/>

</do>

</p></card></wml>
```

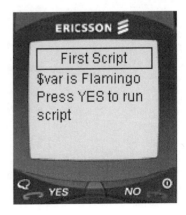

Using Pragmas

WMLScript supports the use of pragmas to supply information to the WMLScript compiler at the WAP gateway.

The pragma must be at the start of the file before any functions are declared so that the compiler will read the pragma first.

All pragmas have the keyword "use" to denote the information that is to be used by the compiler.

The most common use of pragmas is to specify the location of an external WMLScript file for use by the local script:

```
use url otherscript "http://www.server/script";
```

The local name must be unique within the WMLScript file.

Access control may be specified using pragmas to determine the domain and path from which access to the script will be permitted.

This example permits access to the script bearing this pragma from any file located in the "docs" directory, or any of its sub-directories, in the domain "box.com" or "www.box.com":

```
use access domain "box.com" path "/docs";
```

Pragmas can also be used to specify meta information with various properties. The "name" property can be used to specify information for the Web servers but will be ignored by the phone:

```
use meta name "Created" "21-February-2001";
```

The meta property "http equiv" will interpret the information as a HTTP header while "user agent" denotes that the information is intended for use by the phone.

Using Operators

This chapter examines the various types of operators available in WMLScript and illustrates their uses with demonstrations of how to manipulate data.

Covers

Chapter Nine

Arithmetical Operators

WMLScript supports all basic binary arithmetical operations as detailed in the table below.

The bitwise operators are included for completeness but are only used in the low-level manipulation of binary numbers and are not generally used in application scripts:

Operator	Operation
+	add numbers or concatenate strings
-	subtract
*	multiply
/	divide
div	integer division
%	remainder
++	increment
- -	decrement
<<	bitwise left shift
>>	bitwise right shift
>>>	bitwise right shift and zero fill
&	bitwise AND
^	bitwise XOR
|	bitwise OR
~	bitwise NOT

It is possible to influence the resulting data type of a division operation by using "div" to create an integer result, or by using "/" to create a floating-point result. This is demonstrated in the example on the facing page.

...cont'd

```
<wml><card id= "card1" title= "Arithmetic">
<onevent type= "onenterforward"><refresh>
<setvar name= "a" value= "10"/>
<setvar name= "b" value= "10"/>
<setvar name= "c" value= "10"/>
</refresh></onevent><p>
$$a is $(a)<br/>$$b is $(b)<br/>$$c is $(c)<br/>
Press YES to run script
<do type= "accept">
<go href= "script3.wmls#arithmetic($(a),$(b),$(c))"/>
</do></p></card></wml>
```

Use brackets to group code for greater clarity, as with (a/3).

```
extern function arithmetic(a,b,c){
WMLBrowser.setVar( "a",(a/3));
WMLBrowser.setVar( "b",(b div 3));
WMLBrowser.setVar( "c",(c%3));
WMLBrowser.refresh();
}
```

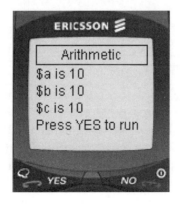

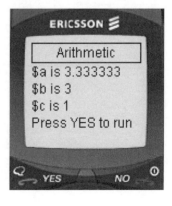

Assignment Operators

WMLScript supports a number of ways to assign values by using the assignment operators set out in the table below:

Operator	Operation
=	simple assignation
+=	add number and assign total or concatenate strings
-=	subtract number and assign
*=	multiply and assign
/=	divide and assign
div=	divide integers and assign
%=	remainder and assign
<<=	bitwise left shift and assign
>>=	bitwise right shift and assign
>>>=	bitwise right shift, zero fill and assign
&=	bitwise AND assign
^=	bitwise XOR assign
|=	bitwise OR assign

The most useful operator after the simple "=" operator is the "+=" operator shown in the example on the facing page.

WMLScript supports automatic type conversion (the operand values are converted automatically to the required data types).

In the example both a and b are initialised with an integer value to which the script assigns additions. The addition of another integer is straightforward. When the script attempts to add a string to an integer the original type is converted to a string to which the additional string is concatenated.

```wml
<wml><card id= "card1" title= "Assignments">
<onevent type= "onenterforward"><refresh>
<setvar name= "a" value= "1"/>
<setvar name= "b" value= "1"/>
</refresh></onevent><p>
$$a is $(a)<br/>$$b is $(b)<br/>
Press YES to run script
<do type= "accept">
<go href= "script2.wmls#assign($(a),$(b))"/>
</do></p></card></wml>
```

Use arguments to pass the current variable values to the function.

```wmls
extern function assign(a,b){
a+=1;
b+= "1";
WMLBrowser.setVar( "a",a);
WMLBrowser.setVar( "b",b);
WMLBrowser.refresh();
}
```

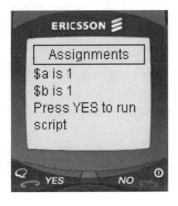

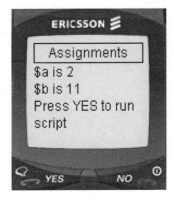

Logical Operators

WMLScript supports the following three logical operators:

Operator	Operation
&&	logical AND
||	logical OR
!	logical NOT

In each case the operator is testing for a match with a boolean "true" state.

With the "&&" operator the WMLScript parser will test to see if both the first and second operands evaluate to "true". If they are both true then the operation itself returns "true", otherwise the operation returns "false".

Note that if the first operand is "false" the operation will return "false" without even testing the second operand because there is then no possibility of matching both.

The "||" operator will test to see if either of the operands evaluates to "true". If the first operand is "true" then the operation will return "true" without even testing the second operand because the match has then already been made.

The "!" operator may be used inversely to test for a "false" state because "not true" is the same as "false".

WMLScript automatically converts the operands to boolean data types for testing and the operation will return "invalid" if no boolean values are present.

The example on the facing page uses all three logical operators to apply a string value to a WMLScript variable if the operations return "true".

In WMLScript the integer values "1" and "0" convert to boolean values of "true" and "false" respectively and can be substituted in the code to replace the "true" and "false" strings.

```
<wml><card id= "card1" title= "Logical"><p>
$$a = $(a)<br/>$$b = $(b)<br/>$$c = $(c)<br/>
Press YES to run script
<do type= "accept">
<go href= "script4.wmls#logic()"/>
</do></p></card></wml>
```

Multiple variables can be declared and initialised following the "var" keyword if they are separated with a comma.

```
extern function logic(){
var a,b,c;
var x=true,y=true,z=false;
if(x&&y)a= "All are true";
if(x||y)b= "One is true";
if(!z)c= "This is false";
WMLBrowser.setVar( "a",a);
WMLBrowser.setVar( "b",b);
WMLBrowser.setVar( "c",c);
WMLBrowser.refresh();
}
```

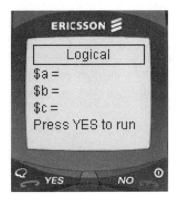

Comparison Operators

All the basic comparison operators found in Javascript are also supported in WMLScript:

Operator	Operation
<	less than
<=	less than or equal to
>	greater than
>=	greater than or equal to
==	is equal to
!=	is not equal to

The operations will return a boolean value of either "true" or "false" unless one of the operands is invalid when the operation itself will return "invalid".

Numeric comparisons are based on the integer and floating point values of the operands.

String comparisons are based on the order of the character codes in the operand strings as defined in the supported character set.

It is possible to make comparisons of boolean values because WMLScript supports the rule that "true" is greater than "false" as attested by the numeric boolean values "1" and "0".

The example below will return true:

```
(3>2)>(3<2)
```

3 is greater than 2 so evaluates to "true".

3 is not less than 2 so evaluates to "false".

So "true" is greater than "false" – the operation returns true.

```
<wml><card id= "card1" title= "Comparison"><p>
$$a = $(a)<br/>$$b = $(b)<br/>$$c = $(c)<br/>
Press YES to run script
<do type= "accept">
<go href= "script5.wmls#comparison()"/>
</do></p></card></wml>
```

```
extern function comparison(){
var a,b,c;
var x=5,y=10,z=20;
if(x<10)a= "less than 10";
if(y==10)b= "exactly 10";
if(z>10)c= "more than 10";
WMLBrowser.setVar( "a",a);
WMLBrowser.setVar( "b",b);
WMLBrowser.setVar( "c",c);
WMLBrowser.refresh();
}
```

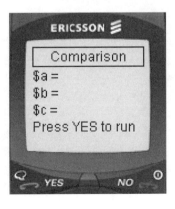
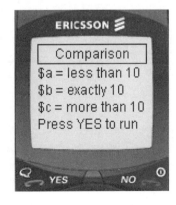

Conditional Operators

The conditional operator "?:" is supported by WMLScript and is most useful because it takes three operands.

The syntax used with the conditional operator is as below:

```
var result = (test) ?  trueAction : falseAction ;
```

This operator evaluates the first operand to determine a boolean "true" or "false" value then selects either the second or third operand based on the evaluation of the first operand.

The result of the operation is then the evaluation of the selected operand.

If the first operand returns "true" then the operator will select the second operand for evaluation.

If the first operand returns "false" then the operator will select the third operand for evaluation.

The third operand will also be selected for evaluation in the event that the first operand returns "invalid".

In the example syntax above the operator evaluates the "test" operand then assigns the value of the appropriate selected other operand to the variable.

The following example uses the conditional operation to determine which of the two functions should be used to assign a value to a variable:

```
<wml><card id= "card1" title= "Conditional"><p>

$$a = $(a)<br/>$$b = $(b)<br/>$$c = $(c)<br/>

Press YES to run script

<do type= "accept">

<go href= "script6.wmls#conditional()"/>

</do></p></card></wml>
```

WLMScript is case-sensitive so "WML" and "wml" are seen as different strings that are not equal.

The expression (z)? is shorthand for (z==true)?

```
extern function conditional(){

var a,b,c;

var x=101, y= "WML", z=true;

a=(x>=100)  ? "100 or more" : "below 100";

b=(y== "wml")?set_one():set_two();

c=(z)?true:false;

WMLBrowser.setVar( "a",a);

WMLBrowser.setVar( "b",b);

WMLBrowser.setVar( "c",c);

WMLBrowser.refresh();

}

function set_one(){

return "one";

}

function set_two(){

return "two";

}
```

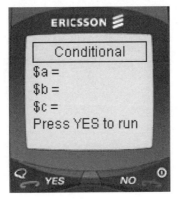

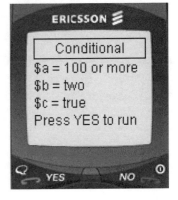

Type Testing

Although WMLScript is a weakly-typed language where the variable types are not rigid, the script does reference the variable values by type and they can be tested for using the WMLScript "typeof" operator.

The operator will return an integer value to describe the data type of the tested value as listed in this table:

Type	Code
Integer	0
Floating-point	1
String	2
Boolean	3
Invalid	4

```
var str= "WMLScript";

var datatype=typeof str;  // datatype = 2
```

The data type can also be verified using the WMLScript operator "isvalid" to return a boolean result as in the following examples:

```
var str= "WMLScript";

var test1=isvalid str; // returns true

var test2=isvalid (1/0); // returns false
```

Making Statements

This chapter discusses the statement blocks within WMLScript functions. You will learn to use conditional branching and how loops can perform in WMLScript.

Covers

Chapter Ten

If-Else

The WMLScript "if" keyword is used to perform an evaluation of an expression to determine its boolean value.

If the evaluation returns "true" then the statement following the expression will be executed.

If the evaluation returns "false" then the statement following the expression is ignored and the script moves on:

```
var sky= "blue";

if(sky== "blue") clouds=0;
```

The conditional test may execute multiple statements if they are grouped in parentheses after the test expression:

```
var sky= "blue";

if(sky== "blue"){clouds=0; rain=false; sunny=true;}
```

A further statement or group of statements may be added for execution in the event that the evaluation returns "false".

This is known as conditional branching and uses the WMLScript keyword "else" to list the optional statements:

```
var sky= "blue";

if(sky== "blue"){

clouds=0; rain=false; sunny=true;

}else{

clouds=1; rain=true; sunny=false;

}
```

WMLScript does not support the "switch" keyword but multiple "if-else" statements can be used as in the example on the facing page.

```
<wml><card id= "card1" title= "If-Else"><p>
$$sky = $(sky)<br/>$$time = $(time)<br/>
Press YES to run script
<do type= "accept">
<go href= "script8.wmls#check_sky()"/>
</do></p></card></wml>
```

```
extern function check_sky(){
var skystate, daytime, sky= "black";
if(sky== "blue"){skystate= "sunny"; daytime= "day";}
else
if(sky== "grey"){skystate= "cloudy"; daytime= "day";}
else
if(sky== "black"){skystate= "darkness";daytime= "night";}
WMLBrowser.setVar( "sky",skystate);
WMLBrowser.setVar( "time",daytime);
WMLBrowser.refresh();
}
```

While

The WMLScript "while" keyword is used to create a loop in which an expression is evaluated for its boolean value.

If the expression returns "true" then the script will execute a statement following the tested expression then loop back to repeat the evaluation.

The loop will continue as long as the expression tested returns "true" but if the test returns "false" or "invalid" the script moves on.

In this example the counter starts at 1 and is incremented by 1 until the counter value reaches 100 when the test expression becomes untrue. At this point the test evaluation returns "false" and the loop ends:

```
var counter=1;

while(counter < 100) counter++;
```

The test expression may evaluate more than one condition and the loop may execute multiple following statements if they are enclosed in parentheses.

In the next example both parts of the test expression must be true for the loop to continue and each iteration of the loop executes both statements enclosed in the following parentheses:

```
<wml>

<card id= "card1" title= "While"><p>

$$color = $(color)<br/>$$counter=$(counter)<br/>

Press YES to run script

<do type= "accept">

<go href= "script9.wmls#do_while()"/>

</do></p>

</card></wml>
```

```
extern function do_while(){
var color= "red";
var counter=1;
while((counter<20)&&(color== "red")){
counter++;
if(counter>15)color= "blue";
}
WMLBrowser.setVar( "counter",counter);
WMLBrowser.setVar( "color",color);
WMLBrowser.refresh();
}
```

When the counter value reaches 15 the test expression still evaluates a "true" response so the statements inside the following parentheses are executed. The counter value is incremented to 16 which then triggers the next statement to execute and set the "color" value to "blue".

As the "color" part of the test expression is no longer now true the loop is broken and the script moves on to set the WML variables and refresh the phone display.

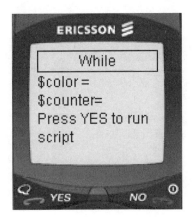 

For

The WMLScript "for" keyword is used to create loops and takes three expressions with the following syntax:

```
for(initialise, test, increment)
```

The intializer declares a starting index value and can be used to declare a new variable for this purpose.

The test can be any expression with a boolean value that will continue the loop while it returns "true" and the increment determines the amount of increase to the index value.

In this example the variable value will change when the counter value is exactly divisible by 25 and so the loop ends:

Notice that the increment is still applied to the index value even though the test is no longer true.

```
extern function do_for(){

var color= "red";

for(var counter=1; color== "red"; counter++){

if(counter % 25 ==0) color= "blue";

}

WMLBrowser.setVar( "counter",counter);

WMLBrowser.setVar( "color",color);

WMLBrowser.refresh();

}
```

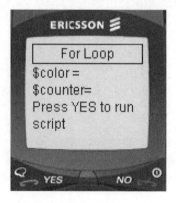

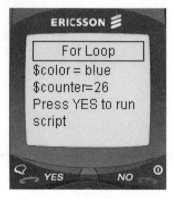

Break/Continue

The "break" and "continue" keywords may only be used in "while" and "for" loops and allow conditional interruption of the loop iteration.

In this "break" example the loop is broken when the counter value reaches 3 and the "if" evaluation returns "true":

```
var marker=0;

for(var counter=0; counter<5; counter++){

if(counter==3)break;

marker++;

}
```

The "continue" keyword is used in the same way as the "break" keyword but does not break the entire loop, only the current iteration of the loop. In the example the marker is not incremented in the iteration when the counter value is 3:

```
var marker=0;

for(var counter=0; counter<5; counter++){

if(counter==3)continue;

marker++;

}
```

Return

The "return" keyword normally returns a result to the caller but can be used to terminate the execution of a function when used as in this example.

The default return value of " " executes at the "if" conditional test without executing the following statements in that function:

```
extern function do_return(){
var color1= "red";
var color2= "green";
WMLBrowser.setVar( "color1",change_color(color1));
WMLBrowser.setVar( "color2",change_color(color2));
WMLBrowser.refresh();
}
function change_color(color){
if(color== "red")return;
else color= "blue";
return color;
}
```

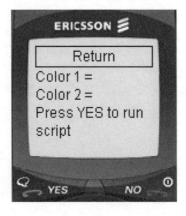
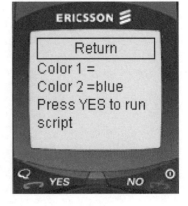

Lang Library

This chapter introduces the WMLScript Lang Library. This is the first of six libraries which are resident in WAP-enabled devices to increase script efficiency. The Lang Library contains functions to extend the core WMLScript language and each function is detailed with examples.

Covers

Chapter Eleven

Min

The "min" function compares two numeric values passed as parameters and has the following syntax:

```
min( value1, value2 )
```

The function will return the lower of the two values.

If the values are equal the function will return the first value and if the arguments are invalid the function will return "invalid".

The example below compares an integer data type number with a floating-point data type number:

To use any library function prefix the function name with its library name followed by a dot.

```
extern function do_min(){

var value1=3;

var value2=2.99;

var result=Lang.min(value1,value2);

WMLBrowser.setVar( "result",result);

WMLBrowser.refresh();

}
```

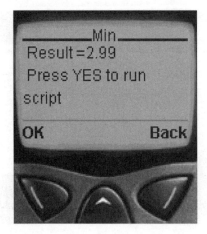

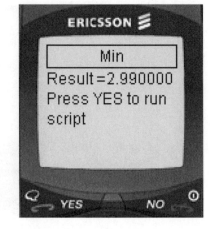

Max

The "max" function compares two numeric values passed as parameters and has the following syntax:

```
max( value1, value2 )
```

The function will return the higher of the two values.

If the values are equal the function will return the first value and if the arguments are invalid the function will return "invalid".

The example below compares an integer data type number with a floating-point data type number:

```
extern function do_max(){

var value1=3;

var value2=2.99;

var result=Lang.max(value1,value2);

WMLBrowser.setVar( "result",result);

WMLBrowser.refresh();

}
```

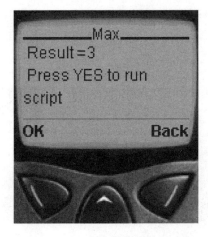
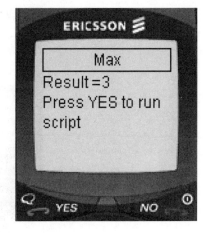

ParseInt

The "parseInt" function examines a string passed as a parameter and has the following syntax:

```
parseInt( value );
```

The function will return the integer value contained within the string argument.

The parser only continues while it meets a digit or leading "+" or "-" and the parsing ends when a non-numeric character is encountered.

The example below parses three strings to extract their integer values:

```
extern function do_parseInt(){

var parse1=Lang.parseInt( "100 only");

var parse2=Lang.parseInt( "2.99 not 3");

var parse3=Lang.parseInt( "only 50");

WMLBrowser.setVar( "result1",parse1);

WMLBrowser.setVar( "result2",parse2);

WMLBrowser.setVar( "result3",parse3);

WMLBrowser.refresh();

}
```

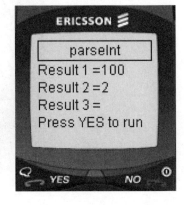

ParseFloat

The "parseFloat" function examines a string passed as a parameter and has the following syntax:

```
parseFloat( value );
```

The function will return the floating-point value contained within the string argument.

Parsing stops when the first character is encountered that cannot be identified as part of a floating-point number.

The example below parses three strings to extract their floating-point values:

```
extern function do_parseFloat(){

var parse1=Lang.parseFloat( "98.6 degrees");

var parse2=Lang.parseFloat( "-50.00 C");

var parse3=Lang.parseFloat( "100");

WMLBrowser.setVar( "result1",parse1);

WMLBrowser.setVar( "result2",parse2);

WMLBrowser.setVar( "result3",parse3);

WMLBrowser.refresh();

}
```

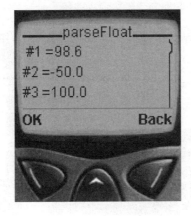
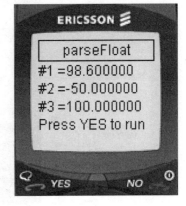

IsInt

The "isInt" function examines a string passed as a parameter and has the following syntax:

```
isInt( value );
```

The function will return a boolean value of "true" if the argument value can be converted to an integer data type.

The function will return "false" for all other data types.

The example below parses three arguments to test for an integer data type:

The floating-point argument will still return "true" because it can be converted to an integer data type.

```
extern function do_isInt(){

var parse1=Lang.isInt( "100");

var parse2=Lang.isInt( "2.99");

var parse3=Lang.isInt( "fifty");

WMLBrowser.setVar( "result1",parse1);

WMLBrowser.setVar( "result2",parse2);

WMLBrowser.setVar( "result3",parse3);

WMLBrowser.refresh();

}
```

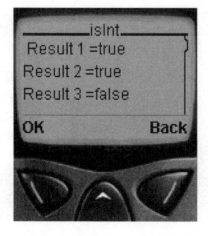

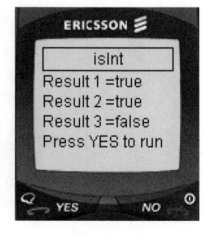

IsFloat

The "isFloat" function examines a string passed as a parameter and has the following syntax:

```
isFloat( value );
```

The function will return a boolean "true" if the argument value can be converted to a floating-point data type.

The function will return "false" for all other data types.

The example below parses three arguments to test for a floating-point data type:

The integer argument will still return "true" because it can be converted to a floating-point data type.

```
extern function do_isFloat(){

var parse1=Lang.isFloat( "0.500");

var parse2=Lang.isFloat( "-500");

var parse3=Lang.isFloat( "#500.00");

WMLBrowser.setVar( "result1",parse1);

WMLBrowser.setVar( "result2",parse2);

WMLBrowser.setVar( "result3",parse3);

WMLBrowser.refresh();

}
```

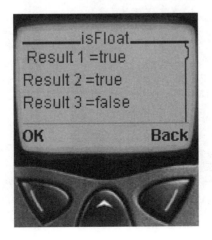

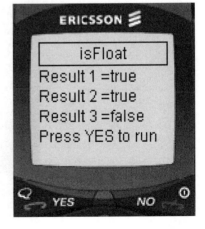

MinInt and MaxInt

WMLScript integer values are 32-bit with a supported range from -2147483648 to 2147483647.

The Lang Library provides a means to get these values at run-time using the library functions minInt() and maxInt().

The example below simply returns the extreme values and uses the maxInt() function to compare a large integer with the maximum supported value:

```
extern function do_minmaxInt(){

var result1=Lang.minInt();

var result2=Lang.maxInt();

var result3=(2147483646<Lang.maxInt())? "true": "false";

WMLBrowser.setVar( "result1",result1);

WMLBrowser.setVar( "result2",result2);

WMLBrowser.setVar( "result3",result3);

WMLBrowser.refresh();

}
```

Abs

The Lang Library abs() function returns the absolute value of a given number.

Integer values are returned when the given number is an integer and a floating-point number is returned when the given number is a floating-point value.

The example passes both integer and floating point numbers and illustrates an invalid given argument:

```
extern function do_abs(){

var result1=Lang.abs(-3);

var result2=Lang.abs(.5000);

var result3=Lang.abs( "fruit");

WMLBrowser.setVar( "result1",result1);

WMLBrowser.setVar( "result2",result2);

WMLBrowser.setVar( "result3",result3);

WMLBrowser.refresh();

}
```

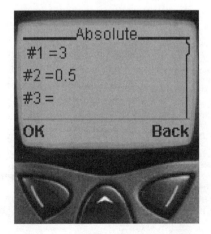 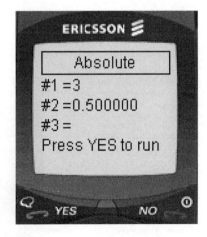

Exit

The WMLScript Lang Library provides the exit() function which may be used to perform a normal exit from a function in cases where the script should be discontinued.

The function requires a string argument or "invalid" to be returned to the WMLScript interpreter and the script execution stops after the exit function is implemented.

The example below uses the exit() function to halt the execution of the do_exit() function so the final variable never receives a set value:

```
extern function do_exit(){

var result1= "alpha",result2= "beta",result3= "gamma";

WMLBrowser.setVar( "result1",result1);

WMLBrowser.setVar( "result2",result2);

WMLBrowser.refresh();

Lang.exit(invalid);

WMLBrowser.setVar( "result3",result3);

WMLBrowser.refresh();

}
```

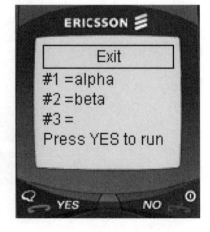

Abort

The WMLScript Lang Library also provides the abort() function which is similar to the Lang.exit() function but may be used to pass an error description to the WMLScript interpreter in cases where the script should be discontinued.

The function requires a string argument as the error description to be returned and the script execution stops after the abort function is implemented.

The example below uses the abort() function to halt the execution of the do_abort() function so the final variable never receives a set value:

```
extern function do_abort(){

var result1= "alpha",result2= "beta",result3= "gamma";

WMLBrowser.setVar( "result1",result1);

WMLBrowser.setVar( "result2",result2);

WMLBrowser.refresh();

Lang.abort("fatal error");

WMLBrowser.setVar( "result3",result3);

WMLBrowser.refresh();

}
```

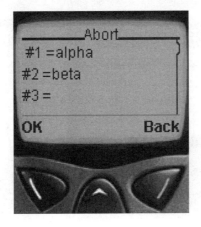

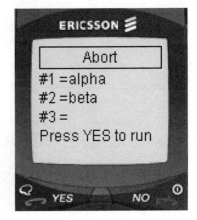

Random

The WMLScript function used to generate random numbers is Lang.random() and takes a single argument to determine the range from which to select a random integer.

The range will be between zero and the argument value.

If the argument is a floating-point type it will be converted to an integer before the random number is selected.

Given values below zero will return "invalid".

The example demonstrates the use of both integer and floating-point arguments to generate a random return:

```
extern function do_random(){

var result1=Lang.random(1000);

var result2=Lang.random(50.00);

var result3=Lang.random(0.75);

WMLBrowser.setVar( "result1",result1);

WMLBrowser.setVar( "result2",result2);

WMLBrowser.setVar( "result3",result3);

WMLBrowser.refresh();

}
```

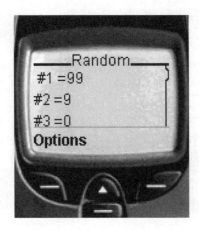
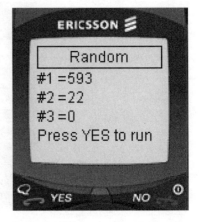

Seed

The WMLScript Lang.seed() function may be used to initialise the Lang.random() function in order to establish a pattern by which to randomise the returned integer.

The seed() function takes a single positive integer argument that is used to initialise the Lang.random() function.

The random() returns will be constant given the same seed value but may differ with platforms as below.

The example shows the seed() function in operation:

```
extern function do_seed(){

Lang.seed(999);

var result1=Lang.random(100);

var result2=Lang.random(50.00);

var result3=Lang.random(-5);

WMLBrowser.setVar( "result1",result1);

WMLBrowser.setVar( "result2",result2);

WMLBrowser.setVar( "result3",result3);

WMLBrowser.refresh();

}
```

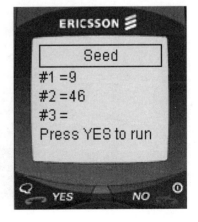

CharacterSet and Float

The Lang.float() library function tests for floating-point support and returns "true" if supported or "false" if not.

The Lang.characterSet() function can be used to test the characterSet supported by the WMLScript interpreter. The function returns an integer value denoting the character set that is supported as in the examples in the table:

Character Set	IANA MIBE number
iso–10646–ucs–2	1000
big5	2026
us–ascii	3
iso–8859–1	4
utf-8	106

```
extern function do_support(){

var result1=Lang.float(); var result2=Lang.characterSet();

WMLBrowser.setVar( "result1",result1);

WMLBrowser.setVar( "result2",result2);

WMLBrowser.refresh();

}
```

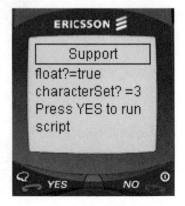

Float Library

This chapter introduces the WMLScript Float Library. This is the second of six libraries which are resident in WAP-enabled devices to increase script efficiency. The Float Library contains functions for arithmetical floating-point calculations and each function is detailed with examples.

Covers

Chapter Twelve

Int

The WMLScript Float Library uses the int() function to return an integer value from a given number.

If the given number is itself an integer value then the return is simply the given number.

Positive and negative values are preserved.

The example illustrates how the int() function is used:

```
extern function do_int(){

var result1=Float.int(3.147);

var result2=Float.int(-200);

var result3=Float.int( "twenty");

WMLBrowser.setVar( "result1",result1);

WMLBrowser.setVar( "result2",result2);

WMLBrowser.setVar( "result3",result3);

WMLBrowser.refresh();

}
```

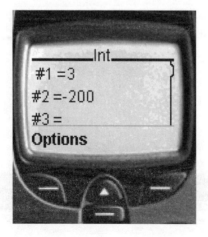
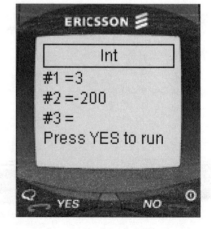

Floor

The Float Library's floor() function rounds down a given number to return an integer value that is nearest to the given number without exceeding its value.

If the given number is itself an integer value then the return is simply the given number.

Positive and negative values are preserved:

```
extern function do_floor(){

var result1 = Float.floor(9.75);

var result2 = Float.floor(9.25);

var result3 = Float.floor(-9.5);

WMLBrowser.setVar( "result1",result1);

WMLBrowser.setVar( "result2",result2);

WMLBrowser.setVar( "result3",result3);

WMLBrowser.refresh();

}
```

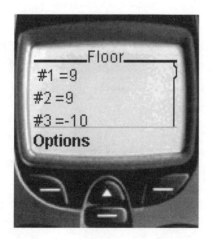

Ceil

The WMLScript Float Library offers the ceil() function to round up a given number and will return an integer that is closest to the given number but not less than its value.

If the given number is itself an integer value then the return is simply the given number.

Positive and negative values are preserved.

This example illustrates the ceil() function in action:

```
extern function do_ceil(){

var result1=Float.ceil(9.75);

var result2=Float.ceil(9.25);

var result3=Float.ceil(-9.5);

WMLBrowser.setVar( "result1",result1);

WMLBrowser.setVar( "result2",result2);

WMLBrowser.setVar( "result3",result3);

WMLBrowser.refresh();

}
```

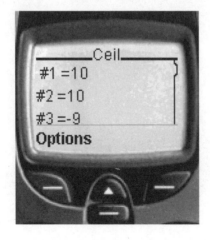
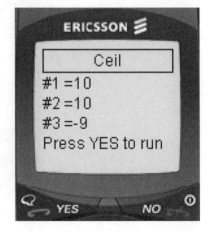

Pow

The Float Library's pow() function takes two arguments and may be used to return the result of raising the first argument to the power of the second argument value:

```
float.pow( value1, value2 );
```

If the first argument has a negative value then the second argument must be an integer.

The value returned is always a floating-point number type:

```
extern function do_pow(){

var result1=Float.pow(12,2);

var result2=Float.pow(12,2.5);

var result3=Float.pow(-12,2);

WMLBrowser.setVar( "result1",result1);

WMLBrowser.setVar( "result2",result2);

WMLBrowser.setVar( "result3",result3);

WMLBrowser.refresh();

}
```

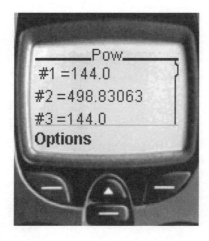

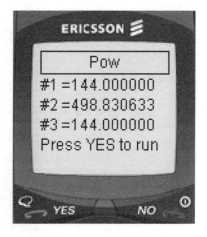

Round

The WMLScript Float.round() function can be used to return a rounded integer value from a given floating-point number.

The return value is the closest integer.

If the given value is exactly halfway between two integers then the function will return the larger integer value.

If the given number is itself an integer value then the return is simply the given number:

```
extern function do_round(){

var result1=Float.round(9.75);

var result2=Float.round(9.25);

var result3=Float.round(2.5);

WMLBrowser.setVar( "result1",result1);

WMLBrowser.setVar( "result2",result2);

WMLBrowser.setVar( "result3",result3);

WMLBrowser.refresh();

}
```

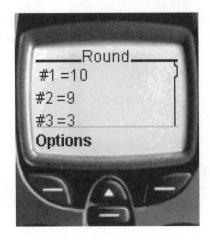
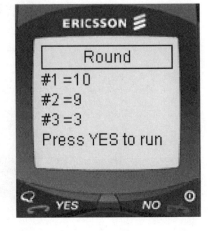

Sqrt

The WMLScript Float Library offers the sqrt() function to return the square root of a given number.

The given number must be a positive value or the function will return "invalid".

The returned value will always be a floating-point number.

This example illustrates the sqrt() function in action using both integer and floating-point given numbers and does not return a result for the negative given number:

```
extern function do_sqrt(){

var result1=Float.sqrt(144);

var result2=Float.sqrt(9.999);

var result3=Float.sqrt(-2.5);

WMLBrowser.setVar( "result1",result1);

WMLBrowser.setVar( "result2",result2);

WMLBrowser.setVar( "result3",result3);

WMLBrowser.refresh();

}
```

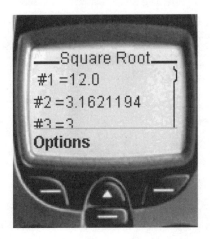
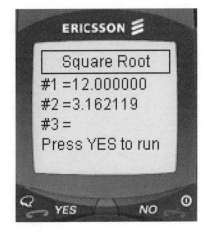

MinFloat and MaxFloat

The final two functions in the WMLScript Float Library are used to return the minimum and maximum values supported by the phone in accordance with the IEEE754 floating-point standard:

```
extern function do_minmaxfloat(){

WMLBrowser.setVar( "result1",Float.minFloat());

WMLBrowser.setVar( "result2",Float.maxFloat());

WMLBrowser.refresh();

}
```

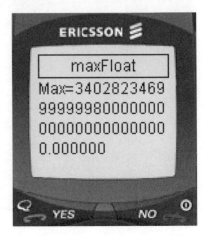

String Library

This chapter introduces the WMLScript String Library. This is the third of six libraries which are resident in WAP-enabled devices to increase script efficiency. A string is an array of characters where each has an index value. The index value of the first character is 0 and the String Library contains functions to manipulate strings.

Covers

Chapter Thirteen

Length

The WMLScript String.length() function takes a single string argument and returns the length of that given string.

Although the character array index starts at 0 the length of the string is returned as the actual number of characters.

Automatic type conversion will be performed to convert non-string values into strings so the length can be counted.

Uninitialised variables contain an empty string by default and return zero as in the example below:

```
extern function do_length(){

var a=String.length( "WMLS");

var b=String.length(911);

var c;

var d=String.length(c);

WMLBrowser.setVar( "result1",a);

WMLBrowser.setVar( "result2",b);

WMLBrowser.setVar( "result3",d);

WMLBrowser.refresh();

}
```

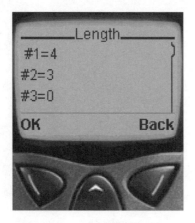

IsEmpty

The String.isEmpty() function performs a test to see if the given argument contains an empty string. The function will return a boolean value depending upon the result of the test.

If the given string is empty the function returns "true" or if a string is found the return will be "false".

The example illustrates that a floating point number undergoes automatic type conversion to a string during the test so that the function will return "false":

```
extern function do_isEmpty(){

var a=String.isEmpty( "WMLS");

var b=String.isEmpty(0.500);

var c;

var d=String.isEmpty(c);

WMLBrowser.setVar( "result1",a);

WMLBrowser.setVar( "result2",b);

WMLBrowser.setVar( "result3",d);

WMLBrowser.refresh();

}
```

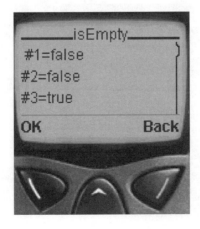
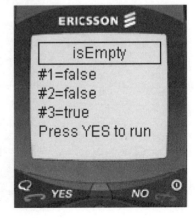

CharAt

The String.charAt() function returns the character at a given position in a given string and takes the test string and index sought as its arguments with the following syntax:

```
String.charAt( string, index );
```

The example shows the function returning the first and last characters of a string:

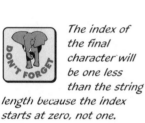

The index of the final character will be one less than the string length because the index starts at zero, not one.

```
extern function do_charAt(){

var str="WMLScript";

var first_char=String.charAt(str,0);

var str_length=String.length(str);

var last_index=str_length - 1;

var last_char=String.charAt(str,last_index);

WMLBrowser.setVar( "result2",str_length);

WMLBrowser.setVar( "result3",last_index);

WMLBrowser.setVar( "result4",last_char);

WMLBrowser.refresh();

}
```

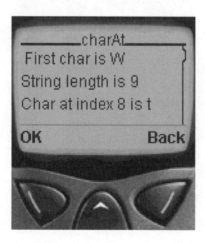

SubString

The WMLScript String.subString() function returns a string selected from a given string and has this syntax:

```
String.subString( string, startIndex, length );
```

The function takes three arguments to specify the given string together with the start index and length of the required return string:

```
extern function do_subString(){

var str= "WMLScript";

var substr1=String.subString(str,0,3);

var substr2=String.subString(str,3,6);

WMLBrowser.setVar( "result1",substr1);

WMLBrowser.setVar( "result2",substr2);

WMLBrowser.refresh();

}
```

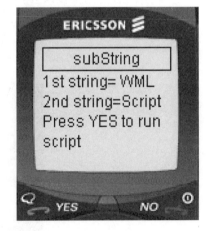

Find

The String.find() function examines a given string to test for a match against a given substring:

```
String.find( string, subString);
```

If a match is successful then the function returns the index value in the given string where the first character of the given substring is located.

If the match fails then the function returns a value of -1.

The function only seeks a single match and no account is made of subsequent matches in the given string:

```
extern function do_find(){

var str="Common Comments";

var match1=String.find(str, "mm");

var match2=String.find(str, "zz");

WMLBrowser.setVar( "result1",match1);

WMLBrowser.setVar( "result2",match2);

WMLBrowser.refresh();

}
```

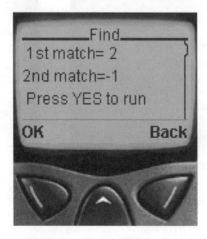

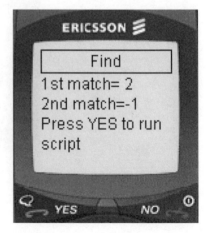

Replace

The String.replace function in WMLScript will examine a given string for occurrences of a given substring:

```
String.replace( string, oldSubString, newSubString );
```

If matches are found the function will replace those substrings with a new given substring in each instance.

The function will return the given string if no matches are found as seen in the example below:

```
extern function do_replace(){

var str= "Offer Baffle";

var match1=String.replace(str, "ff", "tt");

var match2=String.replace(str, "zz", "tt");

WMLBrowser.setVar( "result1",str);

WMLBrowser.setVar( "result2",match1);

WMLBrowser.setVar( "result3",match2);

WMLBrowser.refresh();

}
```

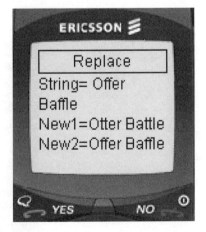

Elements

Strings may contain separator characters to segregate elements within the string. The String.elements() function may be used to return the number of elements separated by the given separator in the given string:

```
String.elements( string, separator );
```

An empty string is still a valid string and will be counted as an element as with the example below which uses the pipe character as a separator:

```
extern function do_elements(){

var str="1|2|34";

var elements1=String.elements(str, "|");

var empty_string;

var elements2=String.elements(empty_string, "|");

WMLBrowser.setVar( "result1",str);

WMLBrowser.setVar( "result2",elements1);

WMLBrowser.setVar( "result3",elements2);

WMLBrowser.refresh();

}
```

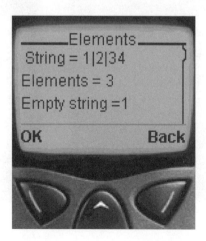

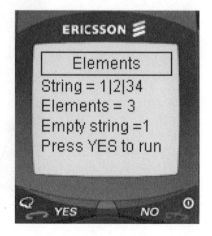

ElementAt

The elements contained in a separated string can be retrieved individually using the String.elementAt() function.

The function takes three arguments to specify the string together with the element index sought and the character that is used as the separator:

```
String.elementAt( string, elementIndex, separator );
```

This example uses a semicolon as the string separator:

```
extern function do_elementAt(){

var str= "1;2;3;4";

var elements1=String.elementAt(str,0, ";");

var elements2=String.elementAt(str,2, ";");

WMLBrowser.setVar( "result1",str);

WMLBrowser.setVar( "result2",elements1);

WMLBrowser.setVar( "result3",elements2);

WMLBrowser.refresh();

}
```

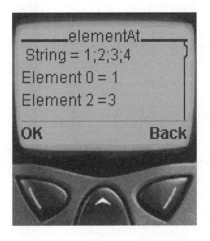
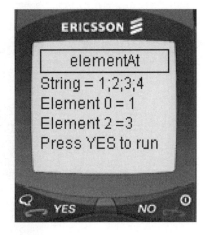

RemoveAt

An element in a separated string can be removed using the String.removeAt() library function which returns a new string with the specified element removed.

The function takes three arguments to specify the string together with the element index sought and the character that is used as the separator:

```
String.removeAt( string, elementIndex, separator );
```

This example uses an exclamation as the string separator:

```
extern function do_removeAt(){

var str= "AAA!BBB!CCC";

var newStr=String.removeAt(str,1, "!");

WMLBrowser.setVar( "result1",str);

WMLBrowser.setVar( "result2",newStr);

WMLBrowser.refresh();

}
```

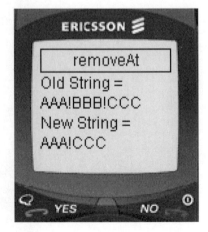

ReplaceAt

An element in a separated string may be changed using the String.replaceAt() function that will replace a specified element then return the new string value:

```
String.replaceAt( string, newElement, index, separator );
```

The function takes four arguments to specify the string and the new element value together with the element index sought and the character that is used as the separator.

This example replaces the third element then returns the new string complete with the new element:

```
extern function do_replaceAt(){

var str= "A@B@C";

var newStr=String.replaceAt(str, "DDD",2, "@");

WMLBrowser.setVar( "result1",str);

WMLBrowser.setVar( "result2",newStr);

WMLBrowser.refresh();

}
```

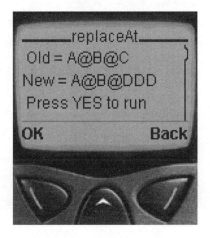

InsertAt

A new element can be added to a separated string with the String.insertAt() library function which will return the new string after the extra element has been added.

The function takes four arguments to specify the string and new element together with the element index sought and the character that is used as the separator:

```
String.insertAt( string, newElement, index, separator );
```

This example adds a new second element:

```
extern function do_insertAt(){

var str= "A|C|D";

var newStr=String.insertAt(str, "B",1, "|");

WMLBrowser.setVar( "result1",str);

WMLBrowser.setVar( "result2",newStr);

WMLBrowser.refresh();

}
```

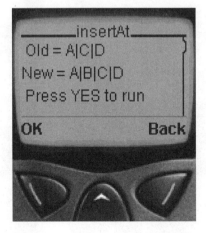
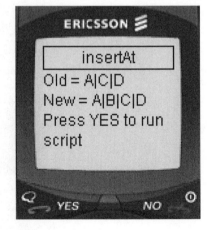

Squeeze

The WMLScript library provides the String.squeeze() function to enable multiple instances of consecutive whitespace to be reduced to just a single space.

The function regards whitespace to be spaces, carriage returns, line feeds and tabs.

This example reduces all spaces to just one space:

```
extern function do_squeeze(){

var str= "A    Z";

var newStr=String.squeeze(str);

WMLBrowser.setVar( "result1",str);

WMLBrowser.setVar( "result2",newStr);

WMLBrowser.refresh();

}
```

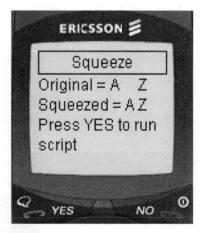

Trim

The WMLScript String.trim() function may be used to trim all trailing and leading whitespaces from a string.

The spaces between characters or words within the string will be unchanged but any whitespace at the beginning or end of the string will be removed.

So the string " One Two Three " will have its leading and trailing spaces deleted to become "One Two Three".

The example trims the leading spaces from the string:

```
extern function do_trim(){

var str= "    ABC";

var newStr=String.trim(str);

WMLBrowser.setVar( "result1",str);

WMLBrowser.setVar( "result2",newStr);

WMLBrowser.refresh();

}
```

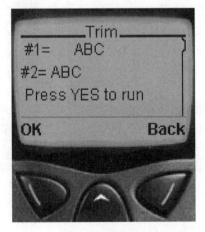

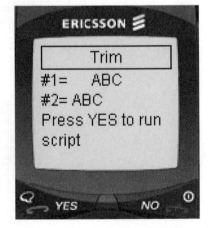

Compare

A string may be compared to another string using the String.compare() function.

The function takes two arguments to specify the strings to be compared:

```
String.compare( string1, string2 );
```

The function returns zero if the strings are found to have identical value. If the string specified in the second argument exceeds the first string then the function will return "1" but if less it will return "-1":

```
extern function do_compare(){

var str1= "BCD";

var str2= "BCE";

var str3= "BCD";

var str4= "ABC";

WMLBrowser.setVar( "result1",String.compare(str1,str2));

WMLBrowser.setVar( "result2",String.compare(str1,str3));

WMLBrowser.setVar( "result3",String.compare(str1,str4));

WMLBrowser.refresh();

}
```

Format

The WMLScript String Library provides the format() function to allow string formats to be specified:

```
String.format( format, string );
```

The format argument is always preceded by a "%".

A positive integer specifies the minimum format size and the function will add blanks before the string to meet this size.

To replace these blanks with zeros a further precision format can be specified prefixed by a dot to distinguish it from the minimum size integer.

The end of the format argument must state a letter to denote the type of format and may be either "d", "f" or "s".

The example below uses the "d" (digits) format type to specify a minimum format size:

```
extern function do_formatWidth(){

WMLBrowser.setVar("result1",String.format("%10d","123"));

WMLBrowser.setVar("result2",String.format("result:%5d","456"));

WMLBrowser.setVar("result3",String.format("%10.10d","789"));

WMLBrowser.refresh();

}
```

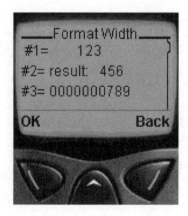
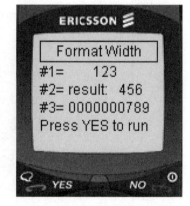

The "f" (floating-points) format type can be used to specify the required format of floating point numbers:

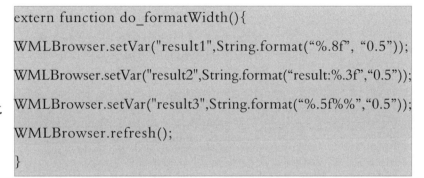

```
extern function do_formatWidth(){

WMLBrowser.setVar("result1",String.format("%.8f", "0.5"));

WMLBrowser.setVar("result2",String.format("result:%.3f","0.5"));

WMLBrowser.setVar("result3",String.format("%.5f%%","0.5"));

WMLBrowser.refresh();

}
```

To include a percentage symbol prefix with another %.

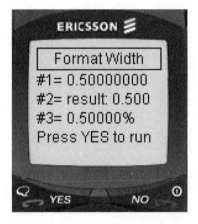

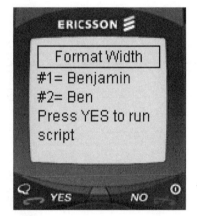

The "s" (string) format type specifies the number of characters and may be used to truncate the string as in the example below:

```
extern function do_formatWidth(){

var str= "Benjamin";

WMLBrowser.setVar( "result1",str);

WMLBrowser.setVar( "result2",String.format( "%.3s",str));

WMLBrowser.refresh();

}
```

ToString

The WMLScript String.toString() function performs the conversion of data types to strings in just the same way that automatic type conversion occurs.

The only difference and advantage is that if the operation fails because the argument cannot be converted to a string type then the function returns the string value "invalid".

In the example the function cannot convert the invalid expression to a string so it returns the string "invalid":

```
extern function do_toString(){

var str1= "WMLScript";

var str2= 1 / 0;

WMLBrowser.setVar( "result1",String.toString(str1));

WMLBrowser.setVar( "result2",String.toString(str2));

WMLBrowser.refresh();

}
```

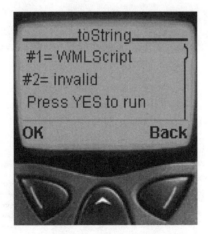

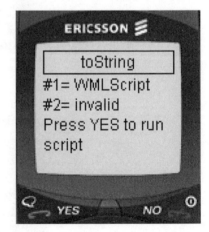

URL Library

This chapter introduces the WMLScript URL Library. This is the fourth of six libraries which are resident in WAP-enabled devices to increase script efficiency. This library contains functions to handle absolute URLs and relative URLs and each function is detailed with examples.

Covers

Chapter Fourteen

IsValid and Resolve

The WMLScript URL Library contains functions to access various parts of a URL address from the general URL syntax:

scheme : // host : port / path ; params ? query # fragment

The URL.isValid() function performs a test on a given URL for conformance to this syntax and returns "true" or "false".

Both absolute and relative URLs can be tested but a relative URL is not automatically resolved into an absolute URL although the URL.resolve() function will achieve this.

```
extern function do_isValidResolve(){

var adr= "http://localhost/xyz.wml";

var bad="?query:http://a.com";

var dom="http://a.com/"; var fil="b.wml";

WMLBrowser.setVar("result1",URL.isValid(adr));

WMLBrowser.setVar("result2",URL.isValid("../xyz.wml"));

WMLBrowser.setVar("result3",URL.isValid(bad));

WMLBrowser.setVar("result4",URL.resolve(dom,fil));

WMLBrowser.refresh();

}
```

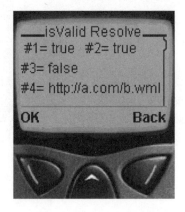
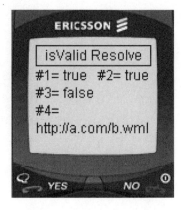

GetScheme, GetHost and GetPort

The WMLScript URL.getScheme() function is used to extract the scheme from a URL while the URL.getHost() function returns the host domain.

If a port is specified in the URL then the URL.getPort() function may be used to retrieve it as in the example.

If no port is specified in the URL then the URL.getPort() function will simply return an empty string.

With each of these functions if an invalid syntax is encountered then that function will return an invalid value:

```
extern function do_getScheme(){

var adr="http://domain.com:80/xyz.wml";

WMLBrowser.setVar("result1",URL.getScheme(adr));

WMLBrowser.setVar("result2",URL.getHost(adr));

WMLBrowser.setVar("result3",URL.getPort(adr));

WMLBrowser.refresh();

}
```

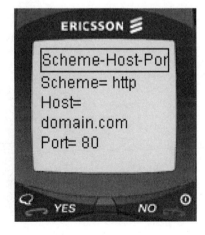

GetPath, GetParameters and GetQuery

The WMLScript URL.getPath() function may be used to extract the path portion of a given absolute or relative URL.

If parameters are included in a given URL they can be extracted using the URL.getParameters() function and a query part of a given URL can be returned using the URL.getQuery() function.

Both getParameters() and getQuery() support relative and absolute URLs and will return an empty string if the given URL does not contain the requested part:

```
extern function do_getPath(){

var adr="http://www.any.com/files/xyz;1;2?a=3&b=4";

WMLBrowser.setVar("result1",URL.getPath(adr));

WMLBrowser.setVar("result2",URL.getParameters(adr));

WMLBrowser.setVar("result3",URL.getQuery(adr));

WMLBrowser.refresh();

}
```

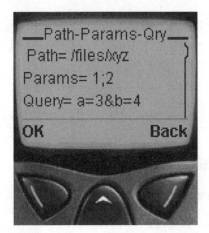

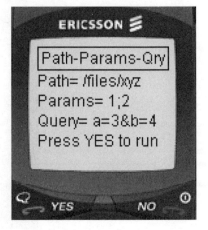

GetFragment, GetBase and GetReferer

The WMLScript URL.getFragment() function returns the fragment part if found in a given absolute or relative URL or will return an empty string if no fragment is present:

```
extern function do_getFrag(){

var adr = "http://www.any.com/files/xyz#abc";

WMLBrowser.setVar("result1",URL.getFragment(adr));

WMLBrowser.refresh();

}
```

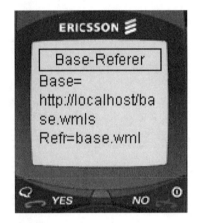

The URL.getBase() function returns an absolute URL of the current WMLScript unit, without a fragment part.

The URL.getReferer() function will return the smallest relative URL of the unit containing the function call:

```
extern function do_getBaseRef(){

WMLBrowser.setVar("result1",URL.getBase());

WMLBrowser.setVar("result2",URL.getReferer());

WMLBrowser.refresh();

}
```

EscapeString

The WMLScript function URL.escapeString() may be used to replace special non-alphanumeric string characters with an escape sequence that will not be processed by the parser.

The escape sequence uses hexadecimal format to replace the special character values and is preceded by a "%" symbol as an identifier.

A space character is also escaped to "%20" and other special characters include:

";" "/" "?" ":" "@" "&" "=" "+" "$" "," "{" "}" "|" "\" "^" "[" "]" "~" "<" ">" "#" "%"

The example depicts some of the special characters with their escaped values:

```
extern function do_escapeString(){

var str= "@#$^<&?%";

WMLBrowser.setVar( "result1", str);

WMLBrowser.setVar( "result2",URL.escapeString(str));

WMLBrowser.refresh();

}
```

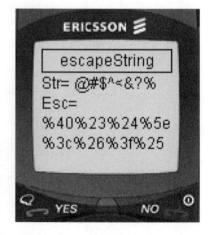

UnescapeString

In order to return escaped strings to regular characters WMLScript provides the URL.unescapeString() function.

Each escaped character that is represented in the hexadecimal format used by the URL.escapeString() function will revert to the standard ASCII format.

The use of escape sequence is most relevant to URL address strings to preserve the non-alphanumeric characters that they contain:

```
extern function do_unescapeString(){

var str= "/d?x=3#crd";

var esc=URL.escapeString(str);

var unesc=URL.unescapeString(esc);

WMLBrowser.setVar( "result1", str);

WMLBrowser.setVar( "result2",esc);

WMLBrowser.setVar( "result3",unesc);

WMLBrowser.refresh();

}
```

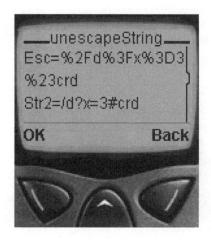

LoadString

A string can be loaded into a variable using WMLScript's URL.loadString() function which has the following syntax:

URL.loadString(url, contentType);

The function will return the content from the given URL with the specified content type.

The content type must have a "text/" prefix but can be any valid sub-type.

If the load fails or if the returned content is not of the specified type then the function will return an error code.

In the example below the function returns the string "mike" from within a text file at the given address:

```
extern function do_loadString(){

var adr= "http://localhost/file.txt";

var str=URL.loadString(adr, "text/plain");

WMLBrowser.setVar( "result1",str);

WMLBrowser.refresh();

}
```

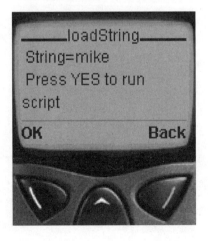

WMLßrowser and Dialogs

This chapter introduces the final two libraries which are resident in WAP-enabled devices to increase script efficiency. The WMLBrowser Library contains functions that allow WMLScript to interact with the WML content and the Dialogs Library contains a set of interface functions.

Covers

Chapter Fifteen

SetVar and Refresh

This library contains functions to access the WML content.

The WMLBrowser setVar() function may be used to allocate a value to a WML variable in associated WML content:

```
WMLBrowser.setVar( variableName, value );
```

If successful the function itself returns "true".

The WMLBrowser.refresh() function updates the display context following execution of the script:

```
<wml><card id= "card1" title= "setVar-Refresh"><p>
Var=$(var)<br/>
Press YES to run script
<do type= "accept">
<go href= "script61.wmls#do_setVarRefresh()"/>
</do></p></card></wml>
```

```
extern function do_setVarRefresh(){
WMLBrowser.setVar( "var",1000);
WMLBrowser.refresh();
}
```

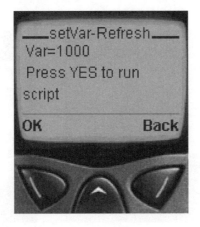
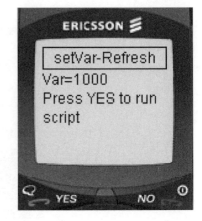

GetVar

The WMLBrowser getVar() function may be used to retrieve the value of a WML variable from associated WML content.

The function will return the value of a variable name passed as an argument unless the variable does not exist when the function will return an empty string.

In the example the first WML variable receives a value from the setVar() function. This value is retrieved by the getVar() function and allocated to a WMLScript variable before setVar() sets the second WML variable value:

```
<wml><card id= "card1" title= "getVar"><p>

Var1=$(var1)<br/>Var2=$(var2)<br/>

Press YES to run script<do type= "accept">

<go href= "script62.wmls#do_getVar()"/>

</do></p></card></wml>
```

```
extern function do_getVar(){

WMLBrowser.setVar( "var1",1000);

var gotVar=WMLBrowser.getVar( "var1");

WMLBrowser.setVar( "var2",gotVar);

WMLBrowser.refresh();}
```

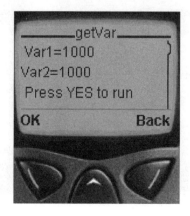
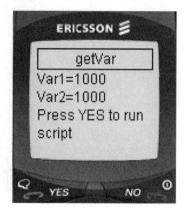

Go

The WMLBrowser.go() function takes a single argument that is a URL that the WMLBrowser should load after the script execution completes.

If the argument is an empty string then no content loads.

The WMLBrowser.go() function works in just the same way as the <GO> task does in WML.

In this example the script determines which URL should load based upon the value passed by the function call:

```
<wml><card id= "card1" title= "Go"><p>

Press YES to run script

<do type= "accept">

<go href= "script63.wmls#do_go(101)"/>

</do></p></card></wml>
```

```
extern function do_go(n){

if(n>=100)WMLBrowser.go( "over100.wml");

else

WMLBrowser.go( "under100.wml");

}
```

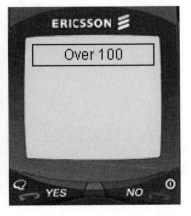

Prev

The WMLBrowser.prev() function instructs the browser to load the previous card after the script execution completes.

The WMLBrowser.prev() function works in just the same way as the <PREV> task does in WML.

In this example the function is called from the second card in a deck and the browser returned to the first card:

```
<wml><card id= "card1" title= "Start"><p>

Press YES for Next Card

<do type= "accept"><go href= "#card2"/></do></p>

</card>

<card id= "card2" title= "Prev"><p>

Press YES to run script

<do type= "accept">

<go href= "script64.wmls#do_prev()"/>

</do></p></card></wml>
```

```
extern function do_prev(){

WMLBrowser.prev();

}
```

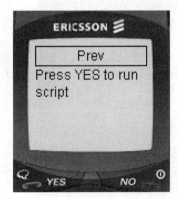
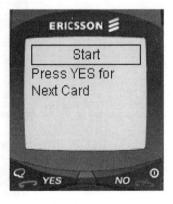

NewContext

The WMLBrowser.newContext() function clears the past browser context so previous history is deleted.

The WMLBrowser.newContext() function works in just the same way as the newcontext attribute does in WML.

In this example the value given to the WML variable is never displayed because the context is renewed thereby losing the variable value of the previous context.

The Ericsson emulator example also loses the card title:

```
<wml><card id= "card1" title= "newContext"><p>

Var=$var<br/>

Press YES to run script

<do type= "accept">

<go href= "script65.wmls#do_newContext()"/>

</do></p></card>

</wml>
```

```
extern function do_newContext(){

WMLBrowser.setVar( "var", "WMLScript");

WMLBrowser.newContext();}
```

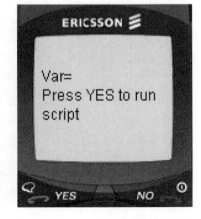

GetCurrentCard

The WMLBrowser.getCurrentCard() function returns the URL of the card currently being processed.

The URL is in relative form unless the deck containing the card does not have the same base location as the script in which case the function will return an absolute URL:

```
<wml><card id= "card1" title= "getCurrentCard">
<do type= "accept"><go href= "#card2"/></do>
<p>Press YES for next</p></card>
<card id= "card2" title= "Card 2">
<do type= "accept">
<go href= "script66.wmls#do_getCurrentCard()"/>
</do><p>Card= $var<br/>Press YES to run script</p>
</card></wml>
```

```
extern function do_getCurrentCard(){
var crd=WMLBrowser.getCurrentCard();
WMLBrowser.setVar( "var",crd);
WMLBrowser.refresh();
}
```

The Ericsson version only returns the URL (and notice that Nokia use the compiled WML file).

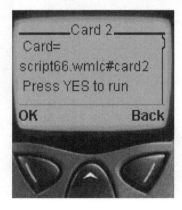

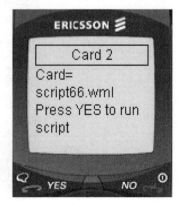

Alert

The Dialogs.alert() library function takes a single argument to be displayed to the user when the function is called.

The message displays on the interface until the user presses a soft key to cancel the dialog in the same way that an alert dialog in a Web browser waits for the user to click OK.

In the example below an alert dialog displays content including data passed by the calling function:

```
<wml><card id= "card1" title= "Alert">
<do type= "accept">
<go href= "script67.wmls#do_alert('Monday')"/>
</do><p>Press YES to run script</p></card>
</wml>
```

```
extern function do_alert(day){
if(day!= "Sunday")Dialogs.alert( "Today is "+day);
}
```

The implementation of dialog boxes may be interpreted in different ways as seen here. The Nokia version does not display the card title when the dialog opens and chooses to display the text content in a bold font automatically.

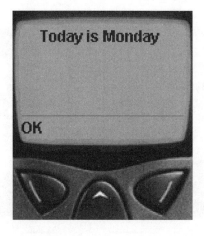
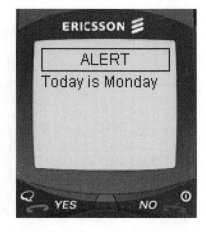

Prompt

The Dialogs.prompt() function is used to display a given message and get input from the user with this syntax:

```
Dialogs.prompt( message, defaultInput );
```

If appropriate the defaultInput argument may be used to provide the user with a value to simply accept or amend. Otherwise this argument can initially be an empty string as in the example below:

```
<wml>
<card id= "card1" title= "Prompt">
<do type= "accept">
<go href= "script68.wmls#do_prompt()"/>
</do>
<p>Press YES to run script</p>
</card>
</wml>
```

```
extern function do_prompt(){
var username=Dialogs.prompt( "Enter first name: ", "");
}
```

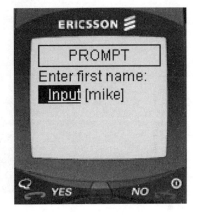

Confirm

The Dialogs.confirm() function will display a message and provide the user with two options before proceeding. If the user selects the first the function returns "true" or the function will return "false" if the second option is chosen.

```
Dialogs.confirm( message, ok, cancel );
```

The example opens an alert dialog if the user selects OK but simply hands back to the browser if Cancel is selected:

```
extern function do_confirm(){

if(Dialogs.confirm("Go ahead?", "OK", "Cancel"))

Dialogs.alert( "OK - Let's Go!" );

}
```

The browser may implement the Confirm dialog in different ways.
Here Ericsson use a select form whereas Nokia allocate the option values to the soft keys for the user's selection.

Convertor Application

This chapter details a sample application to enable currency conversion between the eight leading world currencies. The application uses both WML and WMLScript and the examples illustrate the different way in which two browsers implement the same code.

Covers

Chapter Sixteen

Starting Convertor

The Convertor application starts by loading the first card in the deck which contains a splash-screen. The screen display features a logo if the server locates the WBMP image file and the download has been successful.

The screen will display the ALT attribute if the image does not download or if the user has opted not to display images.

The application title is displayed on the title line and the text content of the card advises the user how to proceed.

The Nokia implementation displays soft key options to return to the previous page or to continue running the Convertor application.

The Ericsson implementation uses the "Yes" soft key to open an Options dialog where the user is presented with the alternatives to return to the previous page or to continue running the Convertor application:

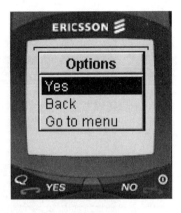

Accepting the option to continue will open a selection page where the user can enter the amount and currency to be converted together with the final currency required.

Nokia have all selections on a single scrollable page but Ericsson allow the user to scroll the current selected values.

In both cases the left soft key opens an input dialog if pressed while the input is highlighted on-screen:

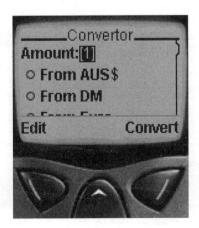 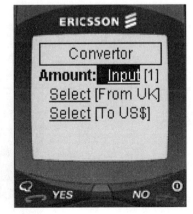

Select Options

The input dialog will accept user input from the keypad in the format specified in the code.

In this example the numeric values of the keys will be used to enter input and the user is wanting to convert US$500 to the equivalent in UK£:

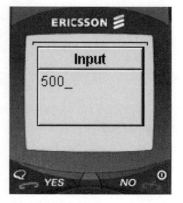

With both browsers the left soft key will enter the input value and return the display back to the selections page.

The Nokia user can now select the type of currency to be converted by scrolling down the options whereas the Ericsson user can scroll down to the selection item then press the left soft key to open the appropriate Options dialog:

The Options dialog in the Ericsson browser will only display all the options to select the type of currency to be converted.

In this example the user scrolls to the option for converting from US dollars then presses the left soft key to select that option:

 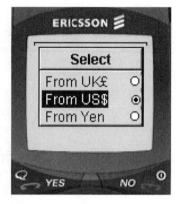

The Nokia browser simply highlights the selection circle to denote that option has been selected.

Ericsson returns to the selections page and shows the newly selected value inside the square brackets for the select item.

Notice that the default value of UK£ has now changed to US$ although the last character is omitted from the display:

Complete Conversion

To select the value of the currency to which the conversion is required the Nokia user just scrolls down to the desired value and presses the left soft key to select that option.

With the Ericsson implementation the left soft key will open the appropriate Options dialog if the user presses the left soft key when the select item is highlighted.

In this example the user will scroll down to the option to convert to UK£ then press the left soft key to select that option:

 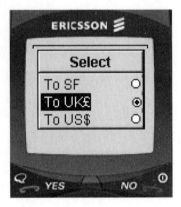

The Nokia browser highlights the selection circle to indicate the selected option and the Ericsson browser returns to the selections page showing the newly selected value:

Now that the required data has been entered and selected the user may make the conversion.

The Nokia implementation has assigned the "Convert" label to the right soft key so the Nokia user can press this key to make the conversion.

Ericsson's implementation assigns the Convert label to the Options dialog which is opened by holding down the left soft key. The user can scroll to the Convert option then press the left soft key to select that option.

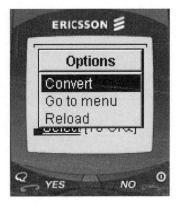

When Convert is selected both browsers display the initial currency type and amount together with the target currency type and equivalent amount:

Convertor WML Code

The following is the entire WML code for the WAP Convertor application and consists of a deck containing three cards.

The first card is the splash-screen page to display the WBMP image, second is the main selections page and the last card is the page displaying the conversion result:

```
<?xml version= "1.0"?>

<!DOCTYPE wml PUBLIC "-//WAPFORUM//DTD WML
1.1//EN" "http://www.wapforum.org/DTD/wml_1.1.xml">

<wml>

<card id= "card1" title= "Convertor">

<do type= "prev" label= "Back">

<prev/>

</do>

<do type= "accept" label= "Yes">

<go href= "#card2"/>

</do>

<p align= "center">

<img src= "curr.wbmp" vspace= "3" alt= "Logo"/>

<br/>

<small>Press </small>

<b>YES</b>

<small> to start</small>

</p>

</card>

<!-- continues -->
```

```wml
<!-- continued -->
<card id= "card2" title= "Convertor">
<do type= "prev" label= "Convert">
<go href="curr.wmls#convert('$(from)','$(to)',$(amt))"/>
</do>
<p>
<b>Amount:</b>
<input name= "amt" value= "1" format= "*N"/>
<select name= "from" value= "STG">
<option value= "AUS">From AUS$$</option>
<option value= "DEM">From DM</option>
<option value= "EUR">From Euro</option>
<option value= "FFR">From FF</option>
<option value= "SFR">From SF</option>
<option value= "STG">From UK£</option>
<option value= "USD">From US$$</option>
<option value= "YEN">From Yen</option>
</select>
<select name= "to" value= "USD">
<option value= "AUS">To AUS$$</option>
<option value= "DEM">To DM</option>
<option value= "EUR">To Euro</option>
<option value= "FFR">To FF</option>
<!-- continues -->
```

```
<!-- continued -->

<option value= "SFR">To SF</option>

<option value= "STG">To UK£</option>

<option value= "USD">To US$$</option>

<option value= "YEN">To Yen</option>

</select>

</p>

</card>


<card id= "card3" title= "Conversion">

<do type= "prev" label= "Back">

<go href= "#card1"/>

</do>

<p align= "center">

<b>$(frm) $(sum)<br/>=<br/>$(cur) $(tot)</b>

</p>

</card>


</wml>
```

Convertor WMLScript

The WML code passes the value of three variables to the WMLScript for the two selected currency types and the amount to be converted.

The WMLScript takes the selected value of the original currency and calls up the exchange rates for that currency from another WMLS file.

In that file the script looks up the rate for the selected target currency and passes its value back to the original script file.

Now the script performs the arithmetic to divide the input amount by the exchange rate to arrive at the equivalent value.

Finally the script applies the values of both currencies and amounts to the appropriate WML variables in the third card of the deck and uses the library method WMLBrowser.go() to display the result on the screen.

The following is the entire WMLScript code for the Convertor application starting with a group of pragmas to identify the location of each set of currency exchange rates for all the supported currencies:

```
// filename: curr.wmls

use url ausRate "http://localhost/currAus.wmls";

use url demRate "http://localhost/currDem.wmls";

use url eurRate "http://localhost/currEur.wmls";

use url ffrRate "http://localhost/currFfr.wmls";

use url sfrRate "http://localhost/currSfr.wmls";

use url stgRate "http://localhost/currStg.wmls";

use url usdRate "http://localhost/currUsd.wmls";

use url yenRate "http://localhost/currYen.wmls";

// continues
```

```
// continued

extern function convert(from,to,amount){

var rate;

if(from== "AUS")rate=ausRate#getAus(to);

if(from== "DEM")rate=demRate#getDem(to);

if(from== "EUR")rate=eurRate#getEur(to);

if(from== "FFR")rate=ffrRate#getFfr(to);

if(from== "SFR")rate=sfrRate#getSfr(to);

if(from== "STG")rate=stgRate#getStg(to);

if(from== "USD")rate=usdRate#getUsd(to);

if(from== "YEN")rate=yenRate#getYen(to);


var result=amount/rate;

var resultStr=String.toString(result);

resultStr=String.format( "%.2f",resultStr);

WMLBrowser.setVar( "frm",from);

WMLBrowser.setVar( "sum",amount);

WMLBrowser.setVar( "cur",to);

WMLBrowser.setVar("tot",resultStr);

WMLBrowser.go("#card3");

}
```

Now follow all of the files containing the exchange rates for each currency so that the appropriate rate can be returned to the main script.

Convertor Rates

```
// filename: currAus.wmls
extern function getAus(to){
if( to == "AUS" ) return 1.0;
if( to == "DEM" ) return 0.7989;
if( to == "EUR" ) return 1.563;
if( to == "FFR" ) return 0.2382;
if( to == "SFR" ) return 1.002;
if( to == "STG" ) return 2.613;
if( to == "USD" ) return 1.714;
if( to == "YEN" ) return 0.01572;
}
```

```
// filename: currDem.wmls
extern function getDem(to){
if( to == "AUS" ) return 1.252;
if( to == "DEM" ) return 1.0;
if( to == "EUR" ) return 1.956;
if( to == "FFR" ) return 0.2982;
if( to == "SFR" ) return 1.254;
if( to == "STG" ) return 3.27;
if( to == "USD" ) return 2.145;
if( to == "YEN" ) return 0.01967;
}
```

```
// filename: currEur.wmls

extern function getEur(to){

if( to == "AUS" ) return 0.6398;

if( to == "DEM" ) return 0.5112;

if( to == "EUR" ) return 1.0;

if( to == "FFR" ) return 0.1524;

if( to == "SFR" ) return 0.6413;

if( to == "STG" ) return 1.672;

if( to == "USD" ) return 1.097;

if( to == "YEN" ) return 0.01006;

}
```

```
// filename: currFfr.wmls

extern function getFfr(to){

if( to == "AUS" ) return 4.198;

if( to == "DEM" ) return 3.354;

if( to == "EUR" ) return 6.561;

if( to == "FFR" ) return 1.0;

if( to == "SFR" ) return 4.207;

if( to == "STG" ) return 10.97;

if( to == "USD" ) return 7.195;

if( to == "YEN" ) return 0.06598;

}
```

```
// filename: currSfr.wmls

extern function getSfr(to){

if( to == "AUS" ) return 0.9978;

if( to == "DEM" ) return 0.7972;

if( to == "EUR" ) return 1.559;

if( to == "FFR" ) return 0.2377;

if( to == "SFR" ) return 1.0;

if( to == "STG" ) return 2.607;

if( to == "USD" ) return 1.71;

if( to == "YEN"") return 0.01568;

}
```

```
// filename: currStg.wmls

extern function getStg(to){

if( to == "AUS" ) return 0.3828;

if( to == "DEM" ) return 0.3058;

if( to == "EUR" ) return 0.5982;

if( to == "FFR" ) return 0.09118;

if( to == "SFR" ) return 0.3836;

if( to == "STG" ) return 1.0;

if( to == "USD" ) return 0.6561;

if( to == "YEN" ) return 0.006016;

}
```

```
// filename: currUsd.wmls

extern function getUsd(to){

if( to == "AUS" ) return 0.5834;

if( to == "DEM" ) return 0.4661;

if( to == "EUR" ) return 0.9118;

if( to == "FFR" ) return 0.139;

if( to == "SFR" ) return 0.5847;

if( to == "STG" ) return 1.524;

if( to == "USD" ) return 1.0;

if( to == "YEN" ) return 0.00917;

}
```

```
// filename: currYen

extern function getYen(to){

if( to == "AUS" ) return 63.62;

if( to == "DEM" ) return 50.83;

if( to == "EUR" ) return 99.43;

if( to == "FFR" ) return 15.16;

if( to == "SFR" ) return 63.76;

if( to == "STG" ) return 166.2;

if( to == "USD" ) return 109.1;

if( to == "YEN" ) return 1.0;

}
```

Index